Table Of Contents

Socialization
Puppy Training
Puppy Bonding
Submissive Pee
Playtime
Whining in the Crate
Parvo, Fleas, Kennel Cough, Rabies, Worms
Tips for New Puppy Trainers
Positive/Negative Training Theory

Dog Sitting

Cleaning House
Difficult Dogs, Difficult Clients
Busy Weekends & Holidays
Keeping A Daily Schedule
Barking
Poop
Security
Paperwork
Sick Dogs
Furniture
Chewing Behavior
Pit Bulls
Home Ownership
Traveling Dog Sitters
Storing Dog Food And Property
Dog Parks
Bathing a Dog
Handling a Medical Emergency
Electric Collars
Baby Gates
Doorbell
Separation Anxiety
Older Dogs
Different Dog Breeds
Rough Play
Water Bowls

Marketing

Puppy Training

Housebreaking

Housebreaking is by far the most challenging part of puppy training. It is what separates me from ordinary trainers.

If you go to PetSmart or to a veterinarian's office for an hourly puppy training class, they can't teach you very much about housebreaking. They might refer you to a book or to a video on YouTube, but you're going to have to do housebreaking yourself.

The problem is, most of us are working, or we're very busy during the day, and we don't have the time to take the puppy out as frequently as we should.

I am an expert in housebreaking because I've done it hundreds of times and so for me it's a much smoother process than if this is a client's first puppy. Busy puppy owners are going to make some mistakes that will drag the process on for months instead of weeks.

I have the added benefit of well trained adult dogs in my house as guests of dog sitting.
These well trained dogs give the puppies an example to follow regarding where to pee and poo. So when the puppy sees the adult dogs going in and out of the doggie door, and the puppy smells poo outside in the yard, but not in the house, this is a powerful teaching aid.

Here is my basic plan for housebreaking an 8 week young puppy:

The very first thing I want to do is take the puppy into the fenced backyard and wait for her to pee. She should pee because she came on a car ride to my home and that usually takes an hour or more.

I want her to meet the other dogs in my backyard, and she's going to smell the poo and pee in the backyard from other dogs. After she's gone pee I'm going to bring her into the house and she's going to sit on my couch with me, beside me. This way I can keep a close eye on her.

I believe in letting the dog make the mistake so that I can correct her and teach her. So she's going to get taken in and out of the doggie door until she learns how to do it herself. That is her first major lesson, how to use the doggie door.

So every hour I will take her outside by putting her out through the doggie door and then I will come get her in 10 or 15 minutes. If she figures out how to come inside on her own than great! She has mastered the doggie door and she is in control of her own potty breaks now. With this she is allowed to roam the house with the other dogs.

But if I see a puddle I'm going to get her and bring her to the puddle. I'm going to hold her close to it so she can smell it, but I will not rub her nose in it because that's not healthy and it's really not necessary. But she is close enough to smell it and see it. Then I will hold her and I will scold her loudly No! Then I will put her back outside.

I will use this time that she is outside to clean the mess with Lysol and a mop. If she might come back in from the yard before I'm done cleaning I will close the doggie door or I will simply attach her to a tie-out line that I have at the rear of my yard. This will prevent her from running back in. Now she is outside and she has been scolded for the pee, and she is waiting for me to allow her back inside.

I never want her to see me cleaning because I feel like she has to understand that humans don't like to clean up pee or poop. I am more of a drama actor in this regard because I will raise my voice No! And really really stomp my feet to show displeasure. Dogs don't speak Human, but they understand body language, so you should act very upset and frustrated when they pee inside.

If I am going to the market or to the gym and I'll be gone an hour, and I don't trust the puppy yet, she will go in her crate. As soon as I return, she has to go straight outside. She also has to go outside immediately from waking from a nap. So I have a potty break at midnight, when I allow all the dogs outside in the yard to go pee and then come back in. So the puppy will do this as well. As soon as I wake up the very first thing I do is take the puppy outside and give her 10 minutes to 20 minutes to pee and poop. You will develop your own judgment on this. But always give her plenty of time to poop in the morning.

We are housebreaking a puppy on a three-week time schedule. That means the puppy has to stop peeing in your house within 10 days. If the puppy is still peeing in your house by day 14, you will have to request an additional week of training with the client. I usually don't charge for the extra week but that's up to you.

If your puppy stops peeing inside your house on day 14, that is not a solid housebreaking if you send her home on Day 21. You will probably get a hit and miss condition where the dog is not 100% housebroken. I offer a one week refresher course with all my puppy clients. That means if they go home and the housebreaking is hit-and-miss, the dog can come back for a refresher week with me where we will work on it again.

The challenge is that the dog has learned to not pee in my house but she has not learned to not pee in the new home with the owner. So I have to guide the owner by text message and phone calls and help them duplicate the method I used in my home for housebreaking.

I am always recommending to my clients that they get a doggie door because it's the easiest way to get the dog to manage her own house is breaking. That is not always possible. If the owner does not have a fenced yard she can get an invisible fence or she can get a tie-out line.

When housebreaking a puppy, bad weather is a big concern. Puppies don't like to go out in cold snow or rainy weather. That is when you have to be alert and take the dog out yourself. If possible, you should clear a path in the snow so the dog has less discomfort outside. I usually put them on a leash and walk them outside and I am using the command "Go Pee!" every time I see the puppy pee I am giving her the same command, "Go Pee." I say, "good girl, Go Pee!" This becomes a command to her.

Then in bad weather, either snow or rain, I will take the puppy outside on a leash, usually it will be doing a break in the bad weather. I will stand out there until she goes pee and poop. If the weather is so bad that I can't see if she went pee or poop I just have to trust my instincts. If I make a mistake and she poos inside or pees inside, I'm going to follow the same routine every single time. I will scold her loudly while she is very close to the accident on the floor. I'm waiting for her to cringe or show a shameful behavior. That tells me that she understands that I do not like accidents on the floor. Then I will put her in the exercise pen in the far room while I clean up the mess.

Ideally, you should have a roof enclosure where snow and hard rains cannot disturb the puppy. This roof enclosure will keep the dog area free from heavy snow and rain so the puppy can go outside with the least discomfort.

Like bad weather, diarrhea is another big problem that you have to be aware of. If you change the puppies' diet too much, she will get diarrhea. This is very difficult for the puppy to control. So if you leave the puppy in the crate with diarrhea, she will poop in the crate, and then walk all over and she will need a bath and you will have to really scrub the crate as well.

To avoid this, we want to make sure the diet of the puppy is healthy. The only human food I give a puppy is hot dog slices, baked chicken or turkey with no grease or salt or anything like that. I also will mix a little bit of wet dog food in with the puppies food to give it some flavor. My treats are usually grain-free and very mild on the stomach. Trust your judgment in this area. Once you find a treat that works for you, stick with it. I rarely use human food with a puppy because of the diarrhea risk. But sometimes I get a puppy who is very finicky and does not respond to traditional puppy training treats which can be from 2 calories to 4 calories. That is when I will turn to hot dog slices or baked chicken slices.

If your puppy gets diarrhea, you want to place the puppy in an area like a laundry room but not a crate. This will allow the puppy to poop the diarrhea in one corner of the room and then avoid it. If your puppy is already using the doggie door, you can put the diarrhea puppy near the doggie door so she can get out quickly when she needs to.

If the puppies poop is too loose you might want to dial back on the treats.

We talked already about negative reinforcement, which is the scolding I do when I see an accident in the house and the way I put the dog outside for a timeout is also called negative reinforcement. Negative reinforcement really works in many situations. For example, the reason I don't kill someone who cuts me off in traffic, is because society would reinforce a negative punishment on me in the form of a prison sentence. This negative fear of punishment is remarkably effective in making me a polite and friendly person in public.

Now let's talk about positive reinforcement. The puppy is going to be praised tremendously and dramatically whenever she pees outside or poops outside. As soon as she pees, I don't want to praise her loudly, because I could startle her, and make her stop peeing. So I speak in a very soft tone, like a mother to a infant. I am softly singing, "Good girl, Go Pee Pee, Good Girl." Then when she is completely finished peeing or pooping, I come up and I give her a good affectionate pet and even more praise.

This is vital to the housebreaking game. In fact if I am outside in the yard and I see an adult dog who is already housebroken and that dog is pooping, I will say "Good Boy, Go Poo Poo." The reason I do this, is it should be an automatic praise for any dog, because the puppies are watching me, and I want the puppy to understand that I like dogs pooping outside.

I never use pee pads and you should not either. Sometimes you will get a crazy client who will ask you to train the puppy to use the pee pads. You cannot do this because you are a dog sitter and you can't have some dogs peeing inside and other dogs peeing outside. That just won't work. Plus you don't want to have to pick up the dirty soiled pee pads and all that mess. The only exception to pee pads is if the dog is sick or very old, then the pee pads in the crate is acceptable. But it is never okay for a puppy to pee pad in my house.

Sometimes a client will ask you to train a puppy to ring a bell to notify the owner that she has to go outside to pee. I have never had any real success with this. A puppy is usually 8 to 10 weeks young and this is very complex behavior and I have a bell that attaches to my door knob but I never use it. I want the puppy to manage her own housebreaking independently. That's the advantage of the doggie door. I don't have to let the dog in or out she knows how to go in and out on her own and she knows it's expected of her.

When a puppy has an accident in the home it is important that you clean it up correctly. Some trainers will tell you to use vinegar or non ammonia based cleaning product or some special enzyme that masks the scent of pee. You can forget all of that. I use a commercial size mop bucket and water and Lysol. I do not mix the Lysol in the bucket because that just doesn't work as well. What I do is I ring the mop, then I take a spray bottle of pure Lysol, usually a lemon scent or an orange scent, and I sprayed the mop head with the stream of Lysol. I spray an amount commensurate to the size of the accident. Lysol has its own unique scent and the puppies will understand they are not supposed to be in the house.

I save my plastic grocery bags from the grocery store. I shop at Meijer so I save those bags and that is what I use to pick up poop in my house. So if the puppy poops in my house right now, I go grab one of those used Meijer grocery bags and put it on my hand like a big glove. I use my hand to pick up the poop just like a poop bag only bigger. Then I walk out the back door of my house and 10 feet away from my home is a five gallon bucket with no lid on it. It is near my trash cans. This is my poop bucket. I put it far away from my home because I don't want to smell it. I put it near the trash cans because it's going to be dumped later in the week. I do not have a lid on the bucket because I want to be able to toss the poop bag in there quickly and get back inside and finish up cleaning the mess.

Sometimes it is easier for me to use an old towel to clean up the pee than the mop. If it's a lot of pee i could ruin the entire mop bucket by soaking it up with the mop. So I sometimes use an old towel does soak up the pee and then follow with a mop.

I should say right now that not all dogs can be housebroken.

There are some dogs who just never seem to get it. That is not your fault. You will offer the same level of effort to every dog you train, including offering the free refresher course of an extra week if necessary. But about one dog in 50 dogs is going to fail to be housebroken within three weeks or even four weeks. I know dogs that have spent their entire life resisting housebreaking efforts. These dogs are still lovable and intelligent in other areas of their life but for some reason they will not poop outside or pee outside. Usually these dogs get given up to shelters because most owners are not willing to clean the poop and pee every day. So we must do all we can to make the puppy solidly housebroken.

But I want to put it into your mind that if you do this as a major business you will come across a dog that is unable to be housebroken. At that point you're going to give the client advice based on your experience and judgment, of how they could manage this behavior. I personally do not give refunds if housebreaking does not work. Like I said it's less than one in 50 dogs that has a serious problem and usually it's a condition where, due to inbreeding from the breeder, the dog has no real control over its bladder, or its colon, and that is more a medical issue than a behavior issue.

When you are housebreaking a puppy, you will learn to watch the puppy for signals that she is going to potty soon.

She will suddenly get up off the couch and start walking around, looking for something. Or she will start sniffing the ground. Or she will go stand by the door which is the most obvious cue you could ever see. When you see this behavior, you simply pick her up and either put her through the doggie door, or take her outside yourself. Be sure to give her 10 minutes or even 15 minutes to take care of her business. If you have to, just close the doggie door and keep her outside and give her as much time as is needed to do her thing.

As a boot camp puppy trainer, you are very different from the puppy training in a class that meets once a week.

You specialize in housebreaking, and I want you to become a master of housebreaking. That is what sets me apart from all other trainers. They may be better trainers at me and maybe they have more awards, and maybe they can get their dog to do the merengue dance, but I am a housebreaking expert, and that is what people need the most.

People don't need service dogs, therapy dogs, or specialty dogs, as much as they need a dog who doesn't pee in their house. So your primary task is to become absolute master of housebreaking. All other parts of training are easy and can be done solidly in 2 weeks. But I need three weeks for housebreaking to be solid. There's really no exception to this rule. If you cut corners and send the dog home a few days early, you will start to get calls that complain about hit and miss accidents.

I write a detailed progress report for each puppy who graduates. They also receive the Canine Good Citizen Award, which I will explain in detail, in another section of the book.

In the progress report, I will mention on the first page my general feeling about the dog and her progress. If her main sticking point is with housebreaking, I'm going to mention it, but I'm also going to mention the progress we made, and that she is ready to go home.

If the puppy is not ready to go home and is not fully housebroken, I'm going to request an additional week of time to get her housebreaking stronger. This used to happen frequently when I was a new trainer but now it never happens.

You are a new puppy trainer. So for the sake of your own sanity, I recommend you do one puppy at a time. Do not take two puppies at the same time. It took me over a year to be able to handle two puppies at the same time. They can drive you crazy LOL. You have to plan your puppy schedule carefully. The way I like to do it now is I have one to two puppies in the home for training. If a puppy is housebroken, I can accept a new puppy who is not. But if I have one puppy who has not yet mastered the doggie door, then I should not bring a second puppy in the house.

Puppies frequently chew on stuff that they're not supposed to. If a puppy chews on tree branches, or rocks, or paper, or plastic, this can cause diarrhea. This makes housebreaking even more difficult. Always make sure your puppy is chewing on appropriate chew toys. Hard rubber chew toys, antlers, Kong and other indestructible items are best.

I have had clients travel hundreds of miles to bring their puppy to me for training. Mostly this is for the housebreaking. No one else offers the housebreaking, and so this is your niche, your expertise. Once you master the simple act of housebreaking you will have a skill that very few people will compete with you for. This is the single most important part of puppy training. Master it and everything else seems easy. My email address is in the back of the book, If you have any questions about housebreaking please message me and I will help you.

ᘧ(´ ᵕ `)ᕤ

Leash Walking

Leash walking can be a very difficult task for some dogs. When I am dog sitting, some dogs have been trained to use the harness or the retractable leash. Those are both bad ideas, because they teach the dog to pull.

The Gentle Leader is a special no-pull collar that fits around the dog's muzzle. It can be effective for small dogs under 40 lb, but a dog over 40 lbs has strong neck muscles, and can easily resist the tug of the Gentle Leader.

For this reason, I use the prong collar for any dog that pulls. As a dog sitter, there is no better way to ensure safety than to use the prong collar. In icy weather, a strong dog can easily pull its owner to the ground.

I even have prong collars for puppies. It is best to stop the pulling impulse as a puppy.

When you are walking a dog, never trust that the collar is snug enough. Lots of owners keep the collar very loose, and the dog may try to slip the collar by moving backwards quickly, while you are pulling forward. I can't tell you how many dogs tried to show me this new trick of theirs. It is very unpleasant to chase a dog down the street because the collar was too loose.

If I have two regular dogs, who come to my house frequently, I can walk them together in a group. I can walk up to 4 well-behaved dogs at the same time.

But if a dog is a young puppy, or new to my home, I have to walk them alone, so that they can learn my pattern of walking.

When I'm walking, I start the walk by taking a picture of the dog and texting it to the owner. This helps the owner feel like she is involved in the training process, and she knows that I am walking the dog every day.

Sometimes I walk very early in the morning, and I usually schedule the text message after 9 a.m. so I don't wake anyone up.

If the puppy pees or poops during the walk, I give her lots of praise. That is a huge importance. Do it every single time, with a real feeling of satisfaction and positivity. Smile!

If the puppy is brand new to leash walking, I don't start with the prong collar the first day. This would be too scary for the puppy.

When I walk the puppy on her first day on the leash, I generally make it as pleasant as possible, I let her guide the walk to some degree, and I never jerk on the line or anything like that.

However, if it has been a few days and the puppy is stubbornly resisting to follow me on the walk, I will introduce the prong collar. I am always hyper-aware that the prong collar can injure a dog if used incorrectly. I never correct the dog with a yank on the leash.

I never let a puppy or an adult dog circle behind me on a leash. This would tangle my feet up and cause an unsafe situation. So if a dog tries to do that I will not allow it. I will stiffen my arm so she can't go behind me.

I want a dog to walk with me in a pleasant manner. If the dog is pulling, I will use the prong collar the next walk. If the dog is walking in front of me too closely for safety, I will use my feet to gently or firmly move the dog to my left or right. I do not insist that a dog "heel" or stay near my heel. The dog is free to move in a broad range as long as she is not impeding my progress or circling behind me.

When we cross the street, I like to trot across, like a light jogging. This is to train the dogs to move quickly across the street and thus avoid traffic. For my personal dogs, I have instilled a mild fear of the street, because I always trot through the streets quickly. It is my hope that if the dogs ever find themselves away from me and near a street, that they will instinctively avoid the street and the cars.

I take the dog from my living room area, and into the laundry room area, to prepare for a walk. I have a coat rack on which 10 different leashes are hanging. I have 4 different sizes of prong collars.

But my favorite leash to use for dogs who do not pull a lot, is a leash with a very large carabiner at the end. This carabiner is 3 inches long and it makes it super easy to clip it onto the dog's collar very quickly.

I do not have time to waste in the mornings. I have a lot of dogs to walk, so this speeds things up quite a bit. I don't look for the little tiny loophole ring on a standard collar. I simply clip my carabiner onto any part of the collar and proceed to start the walk.

If I'm walking a dog and the dog is too distracted with squirrels, or interesting smells on the grass, and there's a lot of tugging and misdirection, I may shorten that walk and return home. But if a dog is walking pleasantly and happily, and it's fun, I am likely to walk a little bit farther and enjoy the morning.

Sometimes when I'm training a young puppy, especially in cold weather, I may have to do a little bit of dragging. This is unfortunate but I gently or firmly insist that the dog walk with me.

If I am walking a difficult dog, one who is pulling a lot and is really being difficult on the walk, I will walk a path with the least distractions. That means not on the main road because I certainly don't want passers-by in cars to see me battling with the dog. I like to walk on bridges and narrow walkways that force the dog to walk straight with minimum distractions.

I live in a cold climate. I have to be very mindful of the temperature when I walk the dogs. The smaller the dog, the more vulnerable she is to cold temperature. My feeling is anything below 30 degrees, we should not do a walk. When you walk a dog in cold weather like that in snow, they will get these little balls of ice on their feet. You will notice they are limping. What you should do is grab the paw with your warm hand and hold it to melt the ice ball. If the dog is a strong and tough dog you can also try continuing the walk and letting it melt off naturally.

Today I walked 4 dogs in 16°F. But they were all healthy, strong dogs, with long winter coats, and we walked a shorter route than usual. Safety First.

On the walks I have an obligation to pick up the poop that the dogs leave in public.

Sometimes I walk in the early morning, when the sun is not out. So I can't really see the poop easily. Other times the dog will poop in the middle of the street, when we are crossing or something crazy like that. This morning my dog pooped in a bunch of autumn leaves and although I could smell the poop I simply couldn't find it because of the camouflage. When I am unable to pick the poop up with any practical judgment, I don't forget about it. 99% of the time I will pick up the poop. Now if I am walking and I am far from a trash can, I will drop the poop bag on the sidewalk so that when I return I will pick it up and take it to the nearest trash can.

Never use a prong collar that has loose joints or links.

You don't want the collar to slip off at the worst time, and force you to chase one or more dogs down the street. You should only use your own personal, trusted leashes. Never use a harness, and never use a retractable leash, these are not for professionals.

I use my own leashes all the time, and I put the owners' leashes in a grocery bag with their name on it, in a back room, to give to them when they return for the dog. I use my own leashes only, because I am responsible for the safety of this dog. I trust my leashes because I inspect them daily and I know how old they are.

Never let a puppy chew on the leash. Never let a puppy lunge at a squirrel or a duck or a cat. Never let a puppy growl at a stranger or a strange dog. In these situations you will say loudly, "No!" This is a command that the puppies will learn. The volume of your voice will tell the puppy how big of a rule violation it is.

When I walk dogs on the leash, I always have a carabiner attached to the end of the leash that I am holding. Even if I'm only walking a single dog. The reason for this is twofold. If I need to tie the dog to a telephone pole, or a tree, or a post really fast, the carabiner helps me do that quickly.

The second reason I use the carabiner is because in the unlikely event that the dog gets away from me and starts running down the road, I know that the carabiner is going to snag on something that will stop the dog from running. It will act like an anchor on a boat, and eventually it will drag on something, and stop the dog so I can catch him. Obviously if I'm walking my personal dogs I don't need to do that because they respond to my verbal commands well.

When I walk my dogs I always have a canister of pepper spray in my front pocket. That's because I started dog training in really rough areas near Detroit and Flint. Lots of pit bulls and dangerous dogs in those areas made me want to protect myself and my dogs from an attack by a pit bull I have never been attacked by a pit bull but I have had close calls.

I recommend you carry pepper spray because a pit bull is so fast you will barely have enough time to get the pepper spray out before he's on you. If you do decide to carry the pepper spray I recommend you practice spraying it on various items for target practice. You should also make sure the pepper spray works because sometimes the canister gets old and clogged and stops working.

Regarding off leash training. Not all dogs can be off leash dogs.

I would say about half are capable of handling the responsibility. That doesn't mean that the dogs who can't handle it are bad dogs. It just means they can't be trusted off leash. So if I believe that a dog has the basic awareness, intelligence and maturity to be off leash, I will use my 20-foot leash that I made from some thick rope and a carabiner. I would take the dog to an open meadow, with no cars or streets near by, and no big distractions like cats, or wild animals, etc.

First I will start by calling the dog over and over to "Come" to me. I would use treats if I felt the dog was responsive. I will continue calling the dog with the Come command over and over, until it becomes automatic. If the dog is distracted by a scent in the grass, I will yank on the 20 ft leash. Over time the dog will learn to respond better and better, and then one day I will be feeling like I can trust the dog without the 20-foot leash.

There is nothing more enjoyable to me, than taking my 3 well-trained dogs to an open field, or a forested area, and letting them run off leash. They love it and so do I. I am constantly testing their recall ability by saying, "Come!"

If the dog is slow to Come, or only comes halfway, I will call the dog until I can put her back on the leash and then we will walk for a few dozen yards with her on the leash. Then I will tell her to "Stay Close!" That is a command for me and my dogs, "Stay Close!" It means I want my dogs to stay within visual and audible range.

If a dog runs farther than you can see or hear her, then she's gone until she decides to find you. Don't let that happen to you. Your dog should never leave your visual sight. Your dog should always come when called, and if not then you need to go home, and in your house, with some hot dogs slices, you need to practice the Come Sit Stay commands, over and over, so the dog understands that you expect them to respond quickly, the first time you say it.

You should never repeat your commands, because that implies that it's okay to ignore it the first time.

That is horrible training. You expect a quick response the first time you call the dog, and if you don't get that then you need to practice your commands, and correct the dog with something uncomfortable like a timeout, or a scolding, or even a light smack on the butt.

When I am training a puppy I will send the owner YouTube videos that I make, showing the puppy's progress week to week. Once a week is good to show a quick video of how the dog is walking on the leash, and you could tell the owner what you are working on, and talk about the progress the dog is making.

Like every part of this training book, I want to help you succeed. My email is in the back of the book, please message me if you have issues regarding leash walking that is not covered in this chapter and we will solve the problem together.

ʅ(￣ ₊ ￣)ʋ

Aggression

There are several types of aggression and I hope to discuss each of them in this section.

First I want to say that aggression really does not fit into your whole dog sitting and puppy training program. A puppy is a sponge for information, and if you have an aggressive dog in your home, the puppy can easily learn to be aggressive, or to be fearful of other dogs. Either situation is horrible and unacceptable.

If someone calls you and says that they want your help training an aggressive dog, tell them that you cannot.

You are a puppy trainer, not an aggressive dog trainer. You can't be both. I trained a lot of aggressive dogs when I was a new trainer. I can tell you that my success rate was not very good. Aggression is very difficult, and sometimes impossible, to remove from a dog. As a dog sitter it is very irresponsible for you to have an aggressive dog in your home.

I do not accept pit bulls of any type in my home.

The only exception is if I'm training an 8-week young puppy pit bull, because I know that this pit bull is not dangerous, and that I am going to teach the dog to be very social with other dogs. I cannot accept a pit bull, because experience has taught me that they have a short temper, and while not all of them are aggressive, I can't tell an aggressive one from a non-aggressive one, just by looking at them.

It is irresponsible to trust an owner's assessment of the dog's temperament. I promise you that if you accept a pit bull into your home, you will lose three regular dog customers. If I was a dog sitting customer, and I saw a pit bull in the sitter's house, I would find another sitter.

You should make arrangements with a local kennel to refer pit bulls and aggressive dogs to them. When someone calls me and tells me they have an aggressive dog, I tell them first, that I cannot train that dog.

I tell them that if it was my dog, I would buy an electric collar, and zap him whenever he shows the slightest aggression. I do not like to use the electric collar, but the major exception to that is when I'm dealing with an aggressive dog. I'm trying to save the dog's life, by making them very uncomfortable when they show aggression. We will talk more about the electric collar in another section. And we will also talk about pit bulls in another section because they deserve more than this brief mention.

I do not allow rough play in my home. Dogs and puppies will go out into the yard and start chasing each other around, and it will seem harmless at first, and then it will escalate slowly, until I hear a yelp, or until they are causing so much noise that they get my attention.

In this case I'm going to scold them and put them in a time out.

I have 2 exercise pens in the back room of my home, and the dogs will go in there for 5 to 15 minutes, depending on how often they break this rule. The exercise pens are not crates. They are 2 ft by 3 ft wide, and they are about 4 ft tall, with a gate in the front and an open-top. There is a dog bed in each exercise pen, which I will remove if the dog is destructive (if he is likely to chew and rip up the dog bed.)

I do not allow any rough play in my home, because I don't want to give an injured dog back to its owner. That's the worst. Injuries are going to happen, but I want them to be very rare, and very small. Aggression just makes for an uncomfortable situation, and the dogs I watch are generally very friendly.

If a dog comes to my home, and he's too much for me to handle comfortably,

I will put a star * by his name in my phone contacts, so when that owner calls me the next time, I will politely decline to watch the dog.

I like to be honest, and say that this dog is a little too much for me to handle in this open home environment. Then I will refer the owner to either a kennel or to Rover.com. I know it sounds crazy, that I am sending clients to competing dog sitters. But I am sending them dogs I don't want to deal with. And that leaves my home with just friendly, fun dogs.

So let's say I am re-homing a dog who has some aggression. I put the electric collar on the dog and I wait for the dog to show the minimum premature signs of aggression. That could be a stiffening of the shoulders, a showing of teeth, a growl, or the raising of the back hair.

I give the dog a zap and I am not afraid to do that. I'm trying to save the dog's life. No one is going to adopt a dog who is aggressive. I tell you this because even though my policy is not to take aggressive dogs, sometimes I'm either helping a friend, or I truly love the dog and I want to see him happy and adopted in a loving home. But the standard rule is no aggressive dogs.

When a dog first comes to my home, and the dog is new to my home, having never been there, I have a special technique.

I never introduce the new dog to the group of other dogs while the owner is here. The reason for that is because I can't correct the dogs in front of a client. So I explain to the owner that as soon as they leave, I will introduce the dogs to make sure they play nice together.

When the owner has left, I will take the dog by the leash and bring her into the living room. I will say loudly "Be Nice!"

And I'm talking to both the regular dogs and the new dog. I sound a little bit menacing, with a warning in my tone, because I want to sound like I'm warning them to play nice. Sometimes I will have a leash or a dish rag in my hand and if a dog is too intrusive with its nose, sniffing the butt of the other, or if I see any sign or hint of aggression, I will wack the dog with the dish rag on the butt. Aggression is not something I take lightly. I insist that the dogs get along. Any dog that tests me will be corrected and put in the time-out area.

Another type of aggression you will see is resource guarding.

I cannot give bones or rawhides to the dogs because they will become possessive and try to take it from one another, and that will lead to an altercation. If I give a dog a rawhide treat or bone, I give it to them at night, and I put them in the exercise pen or a crate, so no other dogs can bother them.

Very similar to resource guarding is food aggression.

When I do my feeding, twice a day, I put every dog in their own area, whether that is a crate, or an exercise pen, or behind a baby gate. On busy weekends and holidays, I will also use my bathroom or my laundry room as a feeding area.

I will talk more about feeding dogs in another section titled feeding. But for now let me say that you never feed dogs together without separating them, or you run the risk of food aggression. I used to toss treats on the floor and the dogs would compete and take the treats from the floor but even that would occasionally cause food aggression.

I try to instill a harmonious sense of friendliness with the dogs. So when I hand them a treat I ask them all to sit, and then I give them a treat one at a time. The first dog to Sit gets the treat, so there is a group pressure to respond quickly to my commands.

By making sure that they all get their treat, I am reducing the urge to take a treat from someone else. If I see a dog with his snout in the mouth of another dog, I'm going to scold and correct that dog for being intrusive.

Like I said, an open-home, dog-sitting environment is no place for aggressive dogs. My motto is friendly dogs only. I will accept German Shepherds, Rottweilers and Dobermans on a case-by-case basis. If there's any hint of aggression I will decline to watch the dog. I have a blanket policy of no pit bulls. I grew up in Southern California, and I watched pit bulls kill cats, and other dogs, and I cannot unsee what I saw. They are lethal machines of death, and I can't tell a dangerous one from a mild one.

I would advise you not to say that you are blacklisting pit bulls. You will get pit bull advocates, harassing you by email and by Facebook. Instead, say,

"Friendly Dogs Only." If I have to directly reject a pit bull, I will say to them that my homeowner's insurance does not cover pit bulls.

Some people say, "dogs will be dogs." I say that a dog becomes what we allow them to become. I do not allow aggression in my home. And that includes barking, growling, possessiveness, and rough play. If a dog behaves this way he will get corrected, and he will soon correct his own behavior and learn to play nice.

Sometimes I will get an old dog, that is very cranky. The dog could be partially or totally blind, partially or totally deaf, and this makes the dog feel vulnerable and fearful. This type of old dog is not truly aggressive, but she is going through a difficult stage in her life. Fortunately, I have a spare room in the back with french glass doors.

I put the dog in that room by herself, but she can still see the other dogs. They cannot bother her. Every hour or so I will give her a private time in the fenced yard, without the other dogs. This is an inconvenience to me, but I love dogs and the old ones are special to me. Many times I watch a dog grow up with me and when they get old, which they all do, I give them all the love I can and make them comfortable in their last days.

ϭ(ﾟ・ｪ・ﾟ)ʋ

Basic Commands

Let's talk about basic commands.

These are the main commands I teach during puppy boot camp.
They are **Sit, Stay, Come,** and sometimes **Down.**

The reason I say sometimes Down, is because not all dogs are able to do the Down command at the early age of 8 weeks. I feel like this is a superfluous command, because you have to Stay on the Sit command, so Down is not nearly as necessary as the other 3 commands.

Usually what happens is, I will train the puppy in Sit, Stay, Come, for a week. Then I will attempt the Down command. If the dog catches on, great, we will reinforce this command. But sometimes the dog is simply too small to do a Down command effectively. Puppies are still learning how to use their own body, and some puppies are incredibly small, like the Dachshund or the miniature breeds. I feel like it is not safe to push on their hind legs and force them into a Down position.

So what I do in this situation, I simply reinforce the primary 3 commands: Sit, Stay and Come. It is better to have these three commands super-solid, than to have them sloppy with the addition of a sloppy Down command.

I am on a strict time schedule, as to what I am able to teach a dog in three short weeks. You have to remember that a human child, the smartest animal in the world, takes two years just to do housebreaking.

So I am teaching an 8-week young puppy basic commands, leash walking, socializing, and the all-important housebreaking, in three short weeks. So I have to use my time wisely. The Sit, Stay, Come commands are super important, and so those have to be solid by graduation.

I do these three commands simultaneously, in a routine that is as automatic for me as brushing my teeth. Sit, Stay, Come. It's always in that order and the only difference is that over time, the Stay command gets a little bit longer, as the puppy learns greater patience and focus.

Let's start with the Sit command. I simply hold my treat, usually a 4-calorie tasty treat that is specifically for dog training, I will say "Sit!" And hold the treat above the dog's head, and a little behind his head, forcing her to look straight up and a little backwards. This is uncomfortable to the dog, so she will sit naturally. As soon as she sits, I give her the treat.

If she does not sit, I slowly and gently push on her posterior until she sits, and then say "Sit" and I give her the treat.

I can't say much more about this command. I always reinforce this command, Sit, whenever I give food to the dog. If it's a treat or if it's her regular meal, I ask her to Sit and then I hand it to her. By reinforcing this command all the time, this is by far the most automatic command the dog will learn.

In my training routine, I immediately follow Sit with a Stay command. Now at first this day command is incredibly simple. I simply hold out my hand flat like a stop sign. I say "Stay!" And I freeze all motion.

I stay in this frozen position for just a second, and then I immediately put my hand down to the floor with the treat in it, and I say "Come!" When the dog comes for the treat I say, "Good Girl!"

Immediately I do the Sit command over again. I will do a training routine with a puppy everyday, rain or shine. The typical training session will last 15 minutes.

I often videotape these training sessions, usually once a week, to share with the owners. I simply upload it to YouTube and send the owner the link by text message so they can watch it at their convenience. This way they don't have to use their cell phone data plan to download the video, they can do it when they have Wi-Fi.

If you thought dog training was more difficult than this, you are only half right. We are specifically talking about puppy training here. Basic commands, housebreaking, leash walking, and socializing, that's the total package for a new puppy. In fact, my puppy boot camp more than qualifies for all of the Canine Good Citizen requirements.

As I practice every day with the puppy, I am slowly extending the time the dog can remain in the Stay position.

First, I get the dog to accept standing perfectly still during Stay. Then I slowly will start to move my feet ever-so-slightly, backwards and away from the dog, during the Stay. If the dog makes any movement at all, I say "No No No!" And I do not give a treat. I ask the dog to Sit again, and I ask the dog to Stay. When the dog stays still I give her the treat.

Slowly, over three weeks time, the puppy will develop her patience and impulse control enough so she can stay without moving, while I walk backwards across the room, or even into the next room. If the dog moves before I say the Come command, I say "No No No!" And I ask the dog to Sit and I do not give the dog a treat.

I want to say more about the training routine, but it is very simple and I don't want to over-complicate it.

If you need further examples of the basic commands, you can message me by email, or you can simply visit YouTube, they have some really powerful and effective videos for teaching basic commands.

Let's talk about the Down command. The way this works is, I will put it in the routine right after the Sit command. This way the dog will be in the Down position when I say Stay, and this is easier for the dog to Stay in the Down position.

The Down position is very easy, but not all dogs like to be pressed on their hind quarters. A dog like a corgi is already so low to the ground that the down position becomes unnecessary and impractical.

Here is what you do. When the dog is in the Sit position, you hold the treat in your hand with your palm up, but your palm is closed. You say "Down!" As you are moving your hand down to the ground slowly, so the dog is following the smell of the treat in your hand. She will follow the scent of the treat down to the floor as you gently push on her back tail area, to encourage her to go down. Once she is down on all fours, you can give her the treat by opening your hand.

Some dogs don't like to go Down and so I will use my other hand did gently guide their legs into the position I want them to be. So if their front legs are resisting the Down position, I will use my free hand to gently but firmly help her into the Down position.

You should expect a little bit of resistance at first. Just keep trying it every so often and don't overwhelm her. If you try the Down position once or twice after the first week, she should pick up on it by the third day. Again, there are excellent videos on YouTube that will show you how to do the Down command.

So now your training routine is Sit, Down, Stay, and Come. You would do that over and over, every day, once a day, for 21 days.

It is important that the new owners practice their basic commands everyday. I put this recommendation in the progress report that I give to every owner on graduation day. A dog learns to listen to me, and recognize my voice and mannerisms, but the owner has to practice with the dog everyday until it becomes a regular routine. If the owner is busy or sloppy and does not practice, the dog will get very sloppy in responding to the commands. Then I will get a call that says the dog is not coming when called. And I will ask them if they were practicing the commands everyday and they will say no.

In this society of instant gratification, and Walmart-style customer service, people mistakenly assume that a dog is a product, like a car or a toaster. You cannot complain about a dog's behavior if you did not follow the training advice in the progress report.

I believe that training is a lifelong journey between the owner and the dog. I am just teaching first grade students in the puppy boot camp. But training never stops. The dog is a living creature and she's going to make mistakes, many times in her life. The owner needs to be there to set boundaries, and to show the dog how they should behave. And all of this starts and ends with the basic commands.

I have a dog, Clover, and she is a perfectly behaved dog. But every once in awhile she will respond poorly when I call her using the Come command. If I feel her response is poor, when we get home from the walk, we will go to a private room. I will grab some treats, and I will practice the same training routine I do with the puppies. This is going to reinforce these commands in her mind, and let her know how important they are to me.

I cannot let her response get sloppy, because one day, in a high-stress situation, I may need her to come to me, and I need to know that she is going to come to me. Perhaps she's in the street, and I'm calling her to the sidewalk, or perhaps there is an angry dog nearby, and I'm calling her to me for her safety. She could be trying to fight a raccoon, and I want to call her before things get bloody. Whatever the reason, she needs to know that I mean business, and she has to drop whatever she's doing and come to me.

One little trick I have when training, is I will use standard training treats from the pet store during normal training days. But on a day when I'm going to video the training, I will use tiny hot dog slices. This fresh meat gives the dog the extra attention and focus that makes the videos pop when you see them. Also, if a dog is finicky and is not very interested in the training treats, I will use hot dog slices.

If I am training a very small puppy, like a Sheltie, a dachshund, or a miniature breed, I have to cut the treats in half , to a size of approximately 2 calories a bite. This way the dog doesn't take a long time chewing and swallowing.

What we do with the basic commands is not magic. Anyone can do this. So how is it that I charge $600 a puppy? Well again, most of my magic is the housebreaking. The basic commands is an added benefit. But whether you are housebreaking or teaching basic commands, you have to be on top of things and be present every day. This is where most people slip up.

Most people go to work or school, they have obligations and responsibilities that don't easily allow them to sit with a puppy all day. And so they do the training commands once a week, instead of once a day, and they do the housebreaking for 8 hours a day, and then nothing for 12 hours or more. This leads to a confused puppy, sloppy housebreaking, and sloppy basic commands.

If a puppy is already housebroken, I can teach the basic commands in just two weeks of boot camp.   For that I charge one third less, so $400. This includes the Canine Good Citizen Award at the end of graduation.   I will speak more about the CGC award in another section.

Basic commands are not very difficult. Humans have been teaching basic commands to dogs for over 10,000 years, before written languages. If a caveman can do this, you can do this. Again, you have limitless online resources at your disposal. You can email me, my address is in the back of the book, and I am happy to help you, just message me. And for any basic command all you have to do is Google the basic command and you will see a million eBooks and a million YouTube videos that will explain things in every detail.

Regarding the treats I use, if the puppy is very small I will buy the cat treats at the supermarket because they are only two calories each. They come in Salmon flavor in tuna flavor and the puppies love them. If the dog is older I will get the four calorie treats, these are made by Brands like Blue Buffalo and Train Me! Brand. Once you find a brand that works for you and doesn't give your puppy diarrhea, stick with that treat.

Ꮙ(˘ ⚐ ˘)ง

Socialization

Socialization is an important part of puppy training and adult dog behavior. I know that you can easily think of adult dogs who are poorly socialized. When you encounter these dogs at a dog park, or walking on the leash, they are barking, acting aggressive, they are jumping up and whining and making a real nuisance.

I take socializing very seriously in the training process. Puppies have a tendency towards rough play and dominance. I do not allow that in my home. Everyone plays nice. If I catch a dog doing rough play, he will get a timeout in the exercise pen for 5 to 15 minutes.

I definitely don't want to give a dog back to its owner with an injury, however small. I do not believe in that whole "dogs will be dogs" nonsense. If two dogs don't like each other, they better pretend to like each other for my sake. I don't have the luxury of being aggressive to people I don't like. And neither does the dog.

The very first step of socializing, occurs when the new dog or puppy comes into my home. I never introduce a new dog to my regular group of dogs, while the owner is still here. That is because I can't correct the dog if the owner is standing right there. So I explain to the owner that as soon as they leave, I will slowly introduce the new dog to the group, to make sure everyone plays nice and is friendly.

When the owner is gone, I take the dog and I put her in the living room. I have a dish rag in my hand. I say in a loud and menacing voice, "Be Nice!" This is a warning and it certainly sounds like a dreadful warning. I am warning the dogs in the group, and I'm warning the new dog, to play nice and to be friendly.
If I see any hair raised, any stiff necks, any intrusive snouts into the posterior of another dog, or any hard looks, I take the dish rag and I whack the dog.

I want you to understand the purpose of the dish rag. It is to stop a dog with an uncomfortable response. I am letting the dog know through my body language that violence is unacceptable and that everyone will get along and play friendly. If the dog is small, the dish rag will just smack on the floor in front of her, to get her attention. If the dog is large, I have no problem hitting the dog on the snout with a dish rag. Be careful of the eyes. We are not trying to hurt the dog. We are trying to discourage the dog from acting aggressively. Dogs are territorial. They used to be wolves, and they evolved with a territorial mindset. I have to let them know that I am the alpha and they have to cooperate with me and with the other dogs in the room. There simply is no tolerance for aggression in a dog sitting or a puppy training environment.

Another part of socialization is when we meet friendly strangers on the walks. I will encourage the stranger to pet the dog if they are interested, and I will personally praise the dog after a successful encounter with a stranger.

I do not allow any barking in my home because barking is a sign of mild aggression.

Barking is a warning. It's a threat, and it's very disturbing to the peace of the home. When children or other dogs walk on the sidewalk near my home, some dogs are tempted to bark. I will run outside and say “No Barking!” If they do it again, they will get a timeout in the exercise pen for 5 to 15 minutes. This will impress upon them that there is no barking allowed.

Some ways I encourage socialization is by playing fetch in the yard, and I bring the ropes into the home, and they can play tug-of-war with each other. In the summertime I have a child's wading pool and the dogs love to play in it. I also walk some dogs together on the walks and this creates a special bond.

I also make at least $1,000 a year training therapy dogs. If you see a dog that is very well socialized and friendly, you should talk to the owner about taking the dog to a nursing home and training it to be a therapy dog. This is extra income for you and it's a great way really socialize a dog. The dog will go to a nursing home and be petted by 50 people each visit, nurses and seniors, and it's all very friendly and the dogs just love it. I will discuss therapy dog training in another section of this book.

ᘳ(¯· ᴥ ¯·)ᘰ

Puppy Training

For me, my puppy training program is unique. I only do board and train boot camp for puppies.

The puppy lives with me for 3 weeks, while I teach the puppy housebreaking, and basic commands, which include Sit, Stay, Down, Come, and No. The puppy will learn to walk on the leash correctly. The puppy will be socialized well with other friendly dogs, and while the puppy is in boot camp she will not be allowed to bark, rough play, jump up, whining, or display destructive behavior.

I charge $600 for the 3-month puppy training. Sometimes, if a breeder is referring a client to me, I may give them $100 discount. You should try charging the $600 and see if your clients are okay with that. I totally think it's a fair price and I don't see anyone else teaching housebreaking, so you have a real niche.

Housebreaking takes 3 weeks to be solid. If you try to shorten this time you will get a hit and miss puppy and you will get calls and complaints. 3 weeks is all I need to train 95% of the puppies.

Basically, a puppy is treated just like a regular dog sitting client, in that the routine is the same. The only exception is, I do an afternoon training session with the puppy, where I take the puppy in a private room and I practice Sit, Stay, Come, with the treats for about 20 minutes.

By doing the basic commands every day for the entire 21 days of the training, I have a solidly trained dog who will respond to my commands perfectly. I always make videos of the dogs doing the training well and post them on my Facebook and YouTube as well as share them with the owners.

For housebreaking, I have a doggie door and a fenced yard, so I expect this dog to go outside and pee and poop out there. If she has an accident, I will bring her to the accident so she can smell it. I will not rub her face in it but I will show it to her so she can clearly see it.

I'm looking for a reaction from her. I'm going to scold her and shout at her as if I'm very upset. This drama is important as my body language is telling her that I am very unhappy. Then I put her outside and I close the doggie door so she has to stay out in the yard. If the weather is good she will stay out there for a little bit while I clean up her accident. After about 10 minutes or so I will let her back in and treat her normally.

Usually this is all I need to do to accomplish housebreaking. I give my housebreaking puppies a middle-of-the-night pee break. I simply pick up the puppy and take her outside and we stay out there in the dark until she goes pee. If she doesn't go pee, it doesn't really matter because she's going back in her crate anyway.

Housebreaking is the biggest part of the puppy training by far. The other commands are easy to teach but housebreaking is almost a magical thing.

If a dog pees in my home too much, she will get a limited access to the home. She will be crated and she will only go from the crate to outside. By restricting her movement I am ensuring that she only pees outside.

If a dog gets diarrhea she should be given a free pass for housebreaking until the diarrhea is gone. No puppy can effectively control diarrhea, so you would be punishing her for no good reason.

When the puppy goes outside in my fenced yard, she smells the ghosts of a million previous poops and pees. This is a big clue as to where she should pee. Her other big clue is that she sees all the other adult dogs peeing and pooing outside. And her third and perhaps biggest clue is the way I go crazy when she pees inside. Put all these clues together and the solution is obvious. She needs to pee outside.

When you are walking your puppy on the leash, and she pees or poops, you want to give her so much praise. Bend down and pet her, praise her with a soft voice, but be sure not to startle her while she is peeing or you might stop the flow. As soon as she is finished peeing, you will begin the praise. I like to overpraise because I want to impress on her how happy I am that she's peeing outside.

If a puppy is rough playing, or chewing toys destructively, or barking, or jumping up, I am teaching the dog and important command, "No!"

I will say the "No!" command one time loudly. The volume of my voice will tell the dog how big of a rule violation she broke. If she does not listen to my "No!" command and she breaks the rule again, she will get a timeout in the exercise pen for 5 to 15 minutes.

I do the same punishment every single time, so the dog knows the consequences breaking the rules. Dogs are naturally pack animals so they want to fit in and do what the rest of the dogs are doing.

Dogs become what you allow them to become. If you ever get stuck on teaching a specific command, or housebreaking, YouTube has hundreds of excellent videos on any dog training topic and I encourage you to look there for a popular video that can help.

I am willing to train a puppy that is a year or younger. I cannot train a puppy younger than 8 weeks.

While I don't accept pit bulls in my home, and this usually includes an 8 week young puppy. I don't want to bond to a puppy that will one day become a dog that is not welcome in my house.

You should not take a very small puppy in the cold winter months for housebreaking. You will have a devil of a time getting a tiny dog to go outside voluntarily and pee. They will be trembling too much to release their bowels outside and they will just come inside and as soon as it's warm they will pee or poop in your house.

If a puppy is in your house for the very first night, which I sometimes call "Hell Night", the puppy will be whining a lot in the crate. First you should shout at the puppy and try to get her to calm down just using your voice.

If she is still whining, you should try a squirt bottle of water to distract her. If she still is whining, I will take a dish rag and whack the top of the crate with it. This will startle the dog and she will probably stop whining.

Some dogs whine a lot their first night or two. If a dog is whining so much you cannot sleep, consider putting the crate in a closed bathroom or laundry room, with the door closed. This should muffle the sound.

If a puppy is teething, and nibbling on your furniture and shoes and things she's not supposed to, you will treat it similar to the puppy who has an accident on the floor. You will show her what she chewed up, you will scold her until she looks like she is ashamed or she is regretful, and then you will put her in a time out for 5 to 15 minutes. Usually after the time out, I will bring an over-sized Rawhide or a hard rubber chew toy for the puppy to chew on. I want to take away whatever bad thing she's chewing and replace it with something that's appropriate.

I have pillows stuck under my furniture and behind couches and chairs, and I use 5 gallon buckets as little puppy barriers so that the puppy cannot crawl behind a television cabinet or past a baby gate or anywhere I cannot see the puppy. I am particularly mindful of electrical wires and cords, so I wrap them in heavy rubber tubing, and I use tape to secure any loose wires so they can't get to it.

You should puppy proof your home. No poisons, no disinfectants in their area, no fragile glass that could break and cause injury. Use your best judgment. Childproofing a home is very similar to puppy proofing a home.

Puppy training is a little more complex than what I've written here. But I truly want you to succeed. In the back of this book is my email address. If there is any part of puppy training that you want to ask me about, just send me an email and I am happy to answer your questions and perhaps even share a professional video with you.

ᕙ(¯ ᴗ ¯)ᕗ

Puppy Bonding

Let's talk about bonding with your training puppy.

The puppy is naturally searching for a mother, to teach her what is safe and what is not. To guide her and protect her and give her food. But the puppy's mother is gone now.

You represent the role of parent to the puppy.

When you are training the puppy, you need to have lots of bonding time. These are moments when you are just rubbing the dog's fur, touching the dog and telling her that you love her, and that she can trust you. You are inviting her to feel safe with you. Dogs are pack animals and you are the leader of the pack. You accept the puppy and make her feel accepted.

Sometimes you are going to feel schizophrenic. Because when the dog pees on the floor, you are going to dramatically shout and complain and correct the puppy. And she's going to wonder if you hate her or if you are rejecting her. You are going to wait a few minutes until things calm down, after you correct her, and then you will walk up to her and offer a friendly hand and smile, and let her know with your body language that you love her and that you are her caretaker and parent.

If you are too heavy handed with the puppy, you will notice that she does not trust you completely. If you call her, she might actually go the other way. This means she's more fearful of you than trusting. You need to correct this by building up the trust. Dogs are incredibly forgiving, so if you lose the trust, you can restore it. But just like humans, it takes only a moment to lose trust and then it takes so long to rebuild it.

My advice is to learn exactly how much correction and discomfort you need to apply to change a dog's behavior. Never over-correct and never make the dog feel more pain than is absolutely necessary to change her behavior.

I wish, that in a perfect world, I didn't have to apply discomfort and pain to any dog. But that's not the world we live in. Your clients don't want to do the uncomfortable task of correcting a puppy. They don't want to see how the sausage is made. You want to be careful about the words you use when speaking to the client. You would never send a client a picture of a dog wearing an electric collar.

When I walk the dogs in the morning, I like to take a picture of the dogs and text it to the owners so they know the dog got the daily walk. I usually like to wait for the dog to dip her head low, so the prong collar is not in the picture. I'm not ashamed of the prong collar but it doesn't make for a pleasant picture.

You want to improve the relationship with the puppy by offering her treats, and lots of praise, making her feel relaxed and comfortable.

Your most powerful training technique is positive reinforcement and all that means is praise, affection, snacks, and treating the dog with love and compassion.

Unfortunately, there are certain situations that require a forceful hand and some discipline. After you apply discipline to the puppy, you want to wait until things calm down, usually 5 minutes or so, and then you go up to the puppy and you pet her and you talk nicely to her and you act friendly so that she trusts you.

When a puppy is too young to use the doggie door, and the puppy has recently came to my home, like the first day or two, I like to sit the puppy next to me on the couch. The puppy is unsure about jumping off the couch, so we are sitting together, and while working on the computer or watching TV, I will absentmindedly just pet the puppy. This simple act is puppy bonding, and it tells the puppy that I am her caretaker, like her parent. If I don't do this bonding, she will not accept the discipline and corrections I give her later on.

Right now, a labradoodle puppy is here for training. Yesterday, she made a terrific scene when her owner left her with me. She ran all over the yard, afraid, aggressive, it was crazy.

I put her in her crate, with her leash around her neck, and connected to the door of the open crate. This makes her feel like she can roam around, but not so far that she can get in trouble.

This morning, I fed her, took her outside on the leash to pee, and returned her to her crate. But if she is hiding in the crate, she is not socializing. So I gently removed her from the crate, and sat her beside me on the couch.

Every few minutes, I give her a friendly pet, cheerful, and with love, while saying her name, over and over. This is puppy bonding. Without this, she will not trust me, and no training can be done.

ᘛ(˙ ༝ ˙)ᘚ

Submissive Pee

This problem is one of the most difficult challenges you will face in puppy training.

The worst cases are when the puppy is 6 months to a year young. These puppies have been allowed to get out of disciplinary trouble simply by peeing. They use it as a weapon. If you try to discipline and correct them they will simply pee like a skunk, and you will be distracted by the pee and forced to give them space and not correct them.

First, we will treat the puppy like any other puppy. When he pees inside, he will get corrected and put in the crate. If he pees in the crate, he will be put in a smaller crate. If he pees in the crate still, he will stay in there for longer periods.

When the dog is out of the crate, you don't want to allow him on your furniture in the living room. Keep him confined to a small area where he can go outside if he needs to pee, but he cannot soil the common area like the living room.

When you have a submissive pee puppy, you don't want to look at him directly in the face, or he will get spooked and urinate.

You want to look away when you are addressing him and speak in a calm voice. Even if you're going to correct him, you don't do it until he is outside or in a crate so he cannot pee on you or your home.

This problem is very difficult to solve. The first thing I would suggest is that you go on YouTube and watch all the YouTube videos about submissive pee.

I personally do not have a 100% success rate with this problem. But when I fail to housebreak a puppy who experiences struggles with submissive pee, I can confidently tell the owner that no one can solve this problem. The puppy will grow out of it in a year or two if they follow my advice carefully.

Some clients might think I have failed as a puppy trainer, if I cannot solve the submissive pee problem. I do not see it that way. If you send your child to high school, and the child does not graduate, is the teacher to blame? Of course not.

I never offer or give refunds if a puppy does not successfully housebreak. Especially not a puppy who did not come to me immediately from the breeder. If a puppy goes to a client's home and the client is too cheap or lazy to hire a trainer, of course housebreaking can go wrong. That is their fault not yours. They don't get to screw up a dog in its learning stage as a puppy, and then bring it to me and expect me to make everything sweet again. I will do my absolute best, but there are no guarantees at all, ever.

Some of you might have more dog experience than I do. Maybe someone reading this book right now has discovered an effective solution to the submissive pee problem. I will ask you to share your solution with me, my email address is in the back of the book and I promise I will respond to your message promptly. I look forward to learning from all of my peers, even the new trainers.

One thing I should remind you of is that dogs with submissive pee or any housebreaking problems have a very difficult life ahead of them. Very few people have the patience to clean pee and poo everyday, indefinitely. This dog will probably be bounced from home to home in frustration, until he ends up in a dog shelter, and it just continues from there. No one wants a dog who is not housebroken. So you must do your absolute best to save this dog's life, and housebreak him. Use all of your resources and intelligence to that end. Study, learn, reach out to your dog training peers, watch those YouTube videos, and figure out a solution for the puppy.

If you have a family who really loves their dog, and they are not willing to give up on housebreaking, I love and admire people like that and I want to help them. So I will ask them to try a second training session with me in a month or two. Eventually we are going to wear this dog down and he will pee outside.

ᘓ(˙ ⱺ ˙)ᑘ

Playtime

Next to the Daily walks, play time is the most important activity. Play time is a way for the dogs to relax and burn off youthful energy. Many dogs come to your home feeling nervous or stressful. Play time is a way for you to show them that it's okay to relax and have a good time.

I have several tennis balls, probably 20 or so, and I keep them in a bucket in my home. When these tennis balls get taken outside in the yard and get dirty and muddy, I put them back in the bucket and then wash them all in the washing machine. No dog wants to play with a dirty, muddy, stinky tennis ball.

I have one wall in my living room that I will toss the ball against, like a racquetball wall. The dogs will wait for the ball to bounce off the wall, and then bring it back to me. I will throw it again and again for as long as they are having fun with it.

Playing tennis ball is a great time to video the dogs having fun in your home. This video can be shared with the owners and posted on Facebook and YouTube. People love to see dogs having fun playing.

Bonding is an important part of puppy training. It is one of the top five principles you must comprehend as a puppy trainer. You have to bond with the dog so she trusts you and listens to you when you give commands. To make this bonding strong, you should sit together with the puppy on the couch. You will have her favorite play toys next to her, and maybe a soft blanket for a plush toy. Keep this plush toy away from the other dogs, who will probably chew and rip it up.

I also have a dozen tennis balls on the yard. When I'm out there picking up poo, which is at least two times a day, I will toss the ball to the far side of the yard so the dogs go get it. While they are on the far side, I'm cleaning the near side of dog poop. They have fun and I get the business of cleaning poop done.

When the balls get ripped up and are missing pieces, when the plush toys are ripped up and the stuffing is coming out, or when any hard durable toy is chewed up and in fragments, I always throw that toy away when I find it on the yard.

When I am out cleaning the fenced yard, I imagine that the dog is putting everything in the yard in her mouth. If it's not safe I remove it from the yard. This is called baby proofing the yard, or puppy proofing your home and yard.

Another favorite game I play with the dogs is tug-of-war. I have a couple of long thick ropes, approximately 3 ft long. I will spin these ropes in a circle around me to excite the dog. When the dog bites into the rope, I will gently play tug with the dog. I should warn you that you can easily pull a dog's tooth out of his mouth by playing tug-of-war. Especially a puppy. You want to be very careful when you are pulling on that rope.

Another favorite toy for many dogs is a crushed 2-liter Coke bottle. Flatten it, so the dog can grip it in her mouth. She will chew it happily, and when it's dirty you can throw it away.

When I am playing with the dogs, I am always looking for signs of rough play or aggressiveness. Any growling or aggressive behavior will result in a time-out. I also don't allow humping where one dog is humping another.

When I'm going to leave the home for an hour or so, I like to put on peaceful ambient music. This makes the dog feel like I'm not very far away. This relaxes the dog, because even though the dog is not a fan of music, dogs are experts in reading body language. The ambient music relaxes me, and that is a cue for the dog to relax.

ᘓ(ˉ .ꞁ ˉ)ʋ

Whining in the Crate

This is one of the most frustrating parts of puppy training. This almost never happens with an adult dog. The puppy who comes to your home is recently separated from her mother and the comfort and security of her siblings. This is all very confusing, and when you put her in a crate alone, and then go to sleep at night, it is understandable when she starts whining and crying in the crate. My wife and I call this Hell Night, because we won't get much sleep the first night.

The first thing I like to try, to reduce the stress on the puppy, is to put her crate near the dog bed of another adult dog. The proximity to the other dog is comforting to the puppy and sometimes that is all you need to do to stop the whining.

The first time I come down from upstairs, I have a lot of patience with the dog. So the dog is whining and wakes me up, and I will come down and I will use a loud voice "No!" I may or may not whack my hand on the crate, to use my body language to tell the dog I am very unhappy with this whining nonsense. When the dog is calm and quiet I will go back upstairs.

As soon as the dog is quiet, I will say the command "Quiet!" I'm trying to teach the dog this command.

Another command that I teach all the dogs is "Good Night." At the end of the day, when I am putting some dogs in their crate, and other dogs will sleep on the dog beds, I will turn out the lights and say "Good Night!" Sometimes I will walk by and say Good Night, followed by each dog's name, to make it personal. I am wishing them a pleasant night, a quiet night, a peaceful night.

Any dog that moves around too much and causes a commotion during the night will be put in the exercise pen, in the back room of the dog area. This is usually enough to stop an adult dog from waking you up at night.

As for the puppy, the second time the puppy whines in the crate, I will probably reach for the water bottle. I will spray the puppy in the face with the water and say "No!" Then I will go back to bed and try to sleep again.

The third time the puppy wakes me up, I will come down and I will take a dish rag and I will whack the top of the dog crate violently with the dish rag, while yelling "No!" loudly. This is a dramatic and physical body language message to the puppy, that she needs to be quiet throughout the night. By this point 50% of all puppies will respond to the dish rag on top of the crate and stop whining.

The fourth time the puppy wakes me up, this is becoming tedious and is also becoming a security and safety concern. The problem is if I have a sleepless night, I may not be able to respond correctly to dog emergencies later in the day, because I will be too tired.

My wife drives an hour commute each way along the highway, and if she has poor sleep it could affect her driving, and cause her to crash. I must have quiet in my home, and I don't have an eternal amount of time to get the dog to be quiet.

The next thing I will do if the puppy continues to whine, I will take the puppy out of the crate and hold the collar in one hand. With his head away from me, I will whack his butt with the dish rag until he cries out. Then I will put him back in the crate and go to bed. At this point 90% of all puppies will stop whining.

If the puppy whines again, I will have no choice but to put the puppy in the spare bathroom and close the door. I may or may not leave the light on, depending on the effect on the puppy. If leaving the light on makes the puppy whine and cry even more, I will turn it off.

Usually this Hell Night scenario of whining becomes less and less of a problem each night until by the third or fourth night there is no whining at all.

ᕦ(̄ ᴥ ̄)ʊ

Parvo, Fleas, Kennel Cough, Rabies, Worms

Let's go down the list of possible diseases that a dog can bring to your home.

By far the most scary disease is parvo. Parvo can kill a dog in 24 hours. It is so quick and so fatal it is truly frightening.

If you get parvo in your home or in your yard, you will need to disinfect at a truly surgical level. The parvo virus stays in yards and homes for a very long time, up to a year and it's even resistant to extreme weather.

A puppy with parvo can die within 48 hours. 90% of all puppies who contract Parvo will die. It is truly a fast and deadly disease.

When you get puppies from the breeder, they will have the first and second parvo booster shots at 8 weeks. They will get the final parvo shot at 12 weeks, which would be after your usual training.

Of course your clients are going to get their standard parvo shots. People pay $500 to $1,500 for puppies and they're not going to skip a $40 shot. I am not in the business of checking health records and verifying the clients do their responsibilities and vaccinate their dogs. I have to trust them at some point. If they ask me about the vaccinations, I will tell them that their dog should get the first two rounds of vaccinations before coming to me. I will also explain that all the other dogs in my home are vaccinated.

If you hear of any dog that had parvo and survived, you cannot accept that dog in your home. This dog is a carrier and could infect others. Stay the hell away from any dog that has or ever did have parvo.

As for fleas, I have never had a problem with fleas. I know that sounds crazy because I have 10 dogs in my home on an average day. I just don't get fleas. I don't have any carpet in my home and if you have carpet I recommend you yank that stuff out of the dog area, and replace it with some laminate or linoleum tile. Ceramic tile is too smooth and slippery. Carpet is horrible for a dog business, because it absorbs pee and smells.

I can imagine people having flea infestations if they have carpeted floors. My dogs run regularly through the meadow, almost daily, and they never get fleas. I don't see ticks either. I purchase the flea and tick medicine like a responsible dog owner, but I have yet to really need it. It is there in case I have a problem.

Kennel cough is a vaccination that you can get when your dog goes in for a rabies vaccine. I recommend your dogs get kennel cough vaccine and you should also recommend that to your clients.

But in the end, that is a personal matter between the dog owner and the veterinarian. An owner will sometimes ask you if you require a kennel cough vaccination. You should ask them when they last received one, and if the stay is not for a week or two, recommend they go get the shot.

Always push for good health in the dogs. But never make a requirement for shots at certain times. If you suspect an owner is poor or is neglecting the dogs' health, you will definitely mention something about that. Have that conversation.

Rabies is the standard part of any vaccinations from the vet. But here's the weird thing. Rabies is kind of like bubonic plague, in that it used to be a serious disease, and now is almost extinct. I've never met anyone who came across a rabies dog. You are highly unlikely to see a case of rabies in your whole life as a dog professional. That does not mean you should not get the shots. I get what the veterinarian recommends for my dogs, within reason.

Now we should talk about worms. Dogs usually get worms from eating poop and other rotten stuff in the yard. The worms will start to devour the poop, and if the dog is a poop eater and eats the poop, now he has worms in his belly. You will notice the worms when he poops. You will see the wriggling in the poop.

Obviously the solution here is to keep the yard clean of poop, and to correct the dog who is eating poop, with a firm scolding and a big time out.

Tips for New Puppy Trainers

The first bit of advice I want to give new puppy trainers, is to join dog training groups on social media. Reddit has a good dog training group, and there are many dog training groups you can join on Facebook. When you have a question about puppy training, ask the group for advice in a post. Most dog trainers are friendly and willing to give you helpful advice. There's also a good chance you will make friends among your peers and learn valuable tips on improving your business.

You never have to feel like you are doing this all alone. My email address is in the back of the book, and I truly want you to succeed as a dog professional. If you have any questions you can message me, and I can share my professional puppy training videos with you and give you helpful tips and advice.

My biggest recommendation to the new puppy trainer is to start with one puppy at a time. It takes about a year to master housebreaking. Don't frustrate yourself with two puppies at the same time when you are new. It's not going to go well. All you have to do, to increase my blood pressure and anxiety, is to mention several puppies at the same time. And I am a master at this, but several puppies can be overwhelming.

If you are still learning, your performance will not be good enough to satisfy your clients, and you will get negative reviews from them. Be smart, go slow, master housebreaking and basic commands with one puppy at a time, and then you can think about expanding your business to include two puppies at the same time.

I currently do two puppies at the same time, but I wait until the first puppy is sufficiently housebroken before I begin with the second puppy. I stagger their arrival dates by 10 days or so, giving me the chance to stabilize one dog's behavior before inviting the new untrained puppy. I highly recommend this pattern for your business. But only after you have mastered housebreaking. You should do one puppy at a time for the first year, in my opinion.

Another great source of dog training information is YouTube. All you have to do is search for puppy training and you will see so many videos on YouTube that are helpful. I post hundreds of my training videos on YouTube, and whenever someone messages me in the comments, I will reply to them in a friendly way and try to help them. So you should do the same.

ᕙ(⁻̑ ˍ ⁻̑)ᕗ

Positive/Negative Training Theory

I have studied dog behavior for seven years. I've read countless books and attended many seminars. So many of my friends are dog trainers, breeders, groomers, and other dog professionals, like veterinarians and shelter workers.

I'm going to sum up everything I found useful in all those books and video training courses.

If you want a dog just stop doing something, like peeing on the floor, you have to make it uncomfortable for him to do it. This will cause him to avoid the unpleasantness and change his behavior.

If you want a dog to continue doing something, like peeing outside, you give him praise and treats and hugs, so that he feels pleasure. The dog will want to continue peeing outside so he can receive the positive and pleasant reaction.

This is the entire principle of behavior change. You make it uncomfortable for the dog to break the rules. And when the dog is behaving really well, and doing things correctly, like following the commands, you give him a treat, or praise, or pat him on the head.

If you give a dog a negative punishment for barking, and he barks again later, you have to decide whether to give him the same level of punishment, or slightly more unpleasant. It is important that you do this with compassion and common sense, so as not to shock the dog and lose his trust. Unpleasant doesn't mean terrifying or cruel.

When I am training for basic commands, which I do every single day, I am using treats the dog finds pleasant. Then when I make a final video for the owner, I use real meat treats, like hot dog slices or small pieces of chicken nuggets, that the dog finds super irresistible. Now his cooperation and interest in basic commands has tripled, and he performs so much better, because he is focused on the meaty tasting treats.

If I ask a dog to Sit, and he does not, I will push his butt into the Sit position and we will rehearse the commands until he is performing well. If he simply refuses to perform at all, he goes in his crate for a time out. At this time I will usually train a dog right in front of the crate, so he has no choice but to watch the training from the crate, missing out on the tasty treats, secretly wishing he could eat those treats. This will influence him the next time I invite him to do the commands.

If I feel the dog needs a lot of negative unpleasantness to correct a behavior, I will consider using the electric collar. I don't like to use it, so it is a last resort. If I put that on the dog, it means the dog is either aggressive or destructive. Other trainers use the collar for simple commands as well, but I feel it's too much. Use your judgment and always error on the side of compassion and love for the dog.

There is nothing else you need to know about Behavior Theory. We are not rocket scientists here. Dogs have been trained by humans for 10,000 years. Do you think your ancestors trained dogs with Clicker or positive-only training? Your ancestors were brutal and many puppies died being trained by them. I'm not suggesting you be brutal. I am only pointing out that the way training took place for thousands of years is dramatically different from our modern mindset.

Just keep in mind that if you were a puppy, you would avoid unpleasantness and move towards things you find pleasant. This behavior is to be found in any animal. We all like pleasure, and we all hate discomfort. This is the only tool you will ever need as a dog trainer. Everything else is fluff and distraction. Yes, you can complicate this simple process eternally, but all dog behavior and even all human behavior can be attributed to positive or negative stimulus. I hate things that are unpleasant and I love things that are pleasant.

ᘚ(˘ ⚬ ˘)ʋ

Dog Sitting

Cleaning House

Cleaning house is super important when running a dog business. A dirty house is unacceptable and no one wants to do business in a dirty house. Dogs require constant cleaning of their area.

Whenever a new client is coming for a meet-and-greet, I am going to sweep and mop with Lysol. I will take any floor rugs and throw them in the washer, and I will do my dishes in my kitchen because they have to walk through my kitchen to get to the dog area.

Even though I clean the dog area well, I do not let this new clients in that area. It is too disruptive with the dogs, and I can't really manage their behavior when a stranger is there. What I do instead is I put a baby gate up, and let the client see the dogs briefly, and see the home-like atmosphere, and then I close my barn door that separates my kitchen from my living room, and we continue talking about their dog.

I think the smell of Lysol tells the world that you recently cleaned your house. My nose has become super sensitive from years of working with dogs. I can smell pee before I find it, and I can smell even a small trace of poop on a shoe or a paw.

Lysol is your friend in the dog business. You should always have a few quarts of Lysol on hand. I get either the lemon smelling or the orange smelling one.

I sweep my home with a broom and dustpan. My wife says I should use a vacuum, but I use the broom frequently, and the vacuum takes too much time, emptying the bag, plugging it in, etc. You do what works best for you. But you have to keep your house clean, it is mandatory.

Because I use the broom, and because I have slow aerial fans in every room that keep the air flow moving, my shelves, appliances, and furniture will have some dust on them. I do not have a lot of time to dust every single item in the house. So this may sound crazy to you, but I have a industrial air compressor, the kind the contractors use for power tools. I use my air compressor hose to blow all the dust down from the rafters, and the lighting fixtures, and the ceiling fans. You would be surprised how much dust I can collect with an air compressor hose.

Each room will get a major air hose dusting once a month. But some rooms require more frequent maintenance if the public is visiting you in those rooms.

Your walls should always look clean. You should become friendly with cheerful looking paint colors, don't be afraid to paint your own rooms. It is very hard to clean mud or grime off the walls with this many dogs, but it is easy to paint a room.

I have a commercial mop bucket, Rubbermaid, with a commercial size mop. I do not pour my Lysol into the mop bucket, because of the amount of dirt that I am picking up. Instead I'll throw some Lysol on the floor, so that the distribution is even throughout the house. Then I will use clean mop water to mop each room, while the Lysol is on the floor.

I have a water bottle that I use to wet and wipe counters, desks, and shelves quickly. It is the same water bottle I used to squirt misbehaving dogs when they need a warning.

Your laundry room is going to be very busy. Dog beds, dog towels, dish rags, they all have to be washed frequently. I recommend that you purchase your next washer and dryer from a used appliance store. I pay $200 for a washer or a dryer and they are used Kenmore washers. They come from a college dormitory, they were used for a year and then they were sold as used. I get a one year warranty on them for free. This sure does beat paying $800 or more for a new washer at Home Depot. Trust me you're going to use your washer so much.

Be careful with your laundry detergent. Dogs have sensitive skin, and they have allergies to strong soap detergents. You want a very small amount of detergent so you don't irritate the dog's skin.

You should also be careful when using detergents on the dog feeding bowls or the dog water bowls. Dogs are already finicky eaters sometimes, and if they have a scent of detergent on their bowl, they may not drink or eat from it. Be smart, rinse that stuff really good and use a very small amount of detergent.

Dogs have thick saliva and some dogs are droolers. So if a dog drools in your water bowl or your feeding bowls, you should soak the bowls overnight in water. This will save you time scrubbing the hard saliva plaque off the bowls.

Regarding my dog beds. I take a typical dog bed, and I wrap it in a heavy duty contractor trash bag. I do this for two reasons.

The first reason is because if the dog pees on the bed, I only want the fitted sheet to get peed. The pee should not soak through to the bed. When the puppy pees on the bed, I will remove the fitted sheet, and tossed it in a hamper with a tight lid on it so the smell won't escape. Next, I will take my Lysol bottle and spray a stream of Lysol on the dog bed. Sometimes I will use the fitted sheet that was soiled to clean up the Lysol off the dog bed. Then I will put a new fitted sheet on the dog bed and I'm done.

Whenever I'm about to film a video, I clean my area really good. I am always aware of the image I'm trying to project on Facebook or YouTube. If my house is dirty and I post a video or photos, that is really really bad. So before I do any training videos, or any type of videos, I make sure the house looks good.

If a dog poops on my floor inside my house, of course I will scold the dog and correct the dog, and put him in a time out for 5 to 10 minutes. I save my white plastic grocery bags from Meijer, and I use them as poop bags. I like them because they're bigger than a poop bag. I pick up as much of the poop as I can, and I have a 5 gallon bucket which is 20 yards from my home. The bucket has no lid on it because I want to be able to toss the poop in the bucket quickly and get back to the business of cleaning the accident area with Lysol and mop.

Cleaning the yard is especially important and it will be covered in detail in a different section. You can never neglect the poop in the yard. You must go out there at least daily and sometimes more than once a day. It doesn't matter if it's snowing or raining, you still have to pick up the poop.

I have a hose attachment that fits to my bathroom sink. I use this hose to quickly fill my mop bucket. I also have a special shower head attachment in my bathtub. If a dog has poop or mud on him, I can take the dog into the bathtub and use the shower head the same way a groomer would wash the dog. I do not offer grooming services to my clients. It's too much of a distraction and I don't need the headache.

I use the shower head attachment in the bathroom for many other cleaning tasks. I will take certain floor mats into the tub and wash them and then dry them outside on a fence or something.

Part of a clean house is keeping the grass cut. If you don't keep your grass short, it will be very hard for you to pick up poop among the tall grass. Keep your grass trim.

Sometimes it's easier to paint something than it is to clean it. If your crates are looking dirty and old, take them out somewhere and spray paint them. Dark paint works best for things that collect a lot of grime. I recommend bright colors for walls and darker colors for floorboards and transition and baseboards.

If your house has a dog smell, you need to find it and get rid of it. Febreze is your friend, but you should not mask a scent, you should remove its source. I burn incense occasionally to give the place a better smell.

I allow dogs to sit with me on the couch. I advise you to do the same. You especially want puppies to approach you on the couch because you can keep an eye on them. If a puppy is on the couch, she probably is not going to pee on the couch.

My couch was old about four years ago. But this couch cost $1,500. So I'm not going to rush out and buy a new one, just because of some wear and tear by the dogs. My solution was, I bought vinyl tarps from the local store. I bought them bigger than the couch by a couple feet on each end. My favorite color tarp is silver because it looks best in the photos.

I simply nailed this tarp over my existing couch like some really primitive upholstery. I use screws and nails and so the thing does not move at all. To be honest, I do this about every six months or so and it cost me $20. So when this tarp starts looking old and worn, I will just go get another tarp and nail it on all over again. My couch gets another face-lift for twenty bucks and I don't have to buy a very expensive couch.

You should always have towels and rags on hand in case of a accident. On rainy days, you better have many dog towels ready, to dry the dogs after they come in. A wet dog can shake himself and ruin the paint on your walls and everything else. If the weather is too muddy and rainy, you should just close the doggie door and wait for the weather to improve. My reasoning is, I would rather have a puddle of pee near the door, than to have 10 wet dogs.

I have five gallon buckets that have lids on them, and I use them as trash cans in each room. The reason for the lid is so the dogs can't get inside the trash.

I do not have any carpeting in the home and you should not either. Dogs and carpets do not mix. I have never had a flea problem in my home despite having so many dogs. I believe this is primarily because I don't have carpet. One dog peeing on your carpet will ruin it for years. And flea eggs can live for over a year in your carpet.

If you have carpet in some parts of the home I suggest you replace it with linoleum, laminate or tile. Carpet requires washing and it never quite gets the smell of dog poop and pee out.

When I am disposing of the poop, I put the poop in the poop buckets. When the bucket is full, I will take a kitchen trash bag, and dump the poop from the bucket into the bag and then tie it shut. I never put open poop into a trash can because I don't want to anger the trash man.

You should always stay on top of cleaning your house. This is a very important part of dog sitting. You will definitely lose customers if you have a dirty home.

ᕦ(˙ ̈ ٤ ̈ ˙)ᕤ

Difficult Dogs, Difficult Clients

Let's talk for a moment about difficult dogs. We love all dogs, but we love friendly dogs just a little bit more.

I have already discussed aggression in a different section. Briefly I will say that difficult dogs are going to make you dread your job. They cause you so much stress and headaches. They are always rough playing, trying to dig under the fence, chewing up stuff in the house. And if a dog is in your home as a sitting, you don't have the time or the inclination to train the dog correctly.

In those situations you could approach the owner and talk about what you're seeing. If you are inclined to train the dog, you could offer training. Usually, a dog just has to live with me for 2 to 3 weeks, and I can help him socialize and behave. Most dogs are what I call "wild," in that they are not bad dogs, they are just wild natured.

After the training process they will be more tame. It's like no one ever sat down and showed them the proper way to behave. That's all I do in training. I also have the benefit of the well-behaved dogs in my home. These dogs set a good example for the misbehaving dogs. That example is huge for a pack animal.

So if the dog's behavior is so unpleasant and difficult that I do not want to train the dog or even sit for the dog, I will follow through with the current stay, even if I have to put the dog in a separate room by himself for the remainder of his time with me. I have 2 exercise pens in the back room. A seriously misbehaving and unruly dog would spend much of his time in the exercise pen, with visits to the fenced yard by himself, closely watched.

I don't want to disturb the clients' vacation with bad news about her misbehaving dog. So I will just send them a periodic picture of the dog in the yard, and I may walk the dog as long as I feel it's safe. But the dog will be separated from the other dogs so no fights or bites can happen.

After the seriously misbehaving dog has left my home, I put a asterisk in front of their phone number, in my phone contacts. So the next time they call me, the asterisk reminds me that this dog was previously difficult, and I will politely decline to sit for this dog. I could either say I'm booked and unavailable, but I usually am honest and say the dog didn't do that well here last time, and I will refer them to Rover.com to find a different sitter.

I know what you thinking. Isn't it stupid to refer a dog to a competing local sitter? I don't see it that way. I feel every dog needs a home, but it's not always my home. And if I selectively filter the dogs in my home, I have a much more pleasant environment. No troublemakers. Meanwhile, my competition is accepting almost any dog, and they are dealing with the headaches that a troublesome dog brings.

Some examples of troublesome dogs could be a dog in heat. One lady brings her dog to me every time the dog is in heat, because she doesn't want to deal with the blood on her furniture. So this would be considered a difficult dog, but honestly this is a problem I can handle. Obviously I have to keep this dog separated from any unfixed males. You cannot let your dogs get pregnant while they are in your house! That is rule number one.

And rule number 2 is security of your business. The seriously misbehaving and unruly dog would spend much of his time in the exercise pen, with visits to the fenced yard by himself, closely watched.

I do not open the front door of my home. It is permanently locked and I never open it. My front door has a storm door, which is the second door, and sometimes in the summer I will open it so the dogs can look out the clear glass and see the street outside. But this door is never ever used to come in and out. The reason is, I never want dogs to be able to escape the home.

I have a huge barn door in the center of my home. This barn door separates the kitchen from the living room where the dogs live. The barn door is one of 2 doors they have to pass in order to actually get outside. I love this vestibule system, because it eliminates the risk of escape.

You have to remember that if a dog escapes your home, there's a high likelihood the dog will die. It is very difficult to catch a dog that does not belong to you, a dog who is scared and misses its owner. He's going to run like hell to try to find his owner again. Add that to the risk of traffic fatality, and bad weather, and the dog is likely to die if he escapes your home. So I cannot impress upon you how important security is. If you have a dog who is an escape risk, you definitely don't want that dog to come back. Be smart!

One time I had these tiny chihuahuas, these miniature dogs. They were so small, that they were able to squeeze through the tiny square of the chain link fence! And they did get out that way, but luckily I was experienced enough to catch them before they got far. Those dogs are not safe here, or anywhere, save a kennel. And that's what I would tell them if they ever called back.

Another dog, a German Shepherd, his owner loves to play fetch by throwing the ball high in the sky. So the dog learned to jump really high. And this dog jumped my 6-foot fence and got out! Luckily, the dog returned when I called him, but that dog is no longer allowed in my home.

I hope that you have a lot of personal patience. Dogs will sometimes test you. You have to be firm, but still compassionate, with a gentle insistence on the rules without being a real jerk. If you are not in this business because you love dogs, you're probably in the wrong business.

Let's talk about health problems. These would be classified as difficult dogs but I am okay with providing care for a dog who has had recent surgery, or dog who is very old and incontinent, that's okay I can handle that. Or a dog who is blind, deaf, or needs help walking, I can accommodate that dog.

If a dog is injured in your home, whatever the cause, you need to immediately notify the owners. You'll take a picture of any vomit, or any real bad diarrhea, or any scratch, cut, lesion, whatever it is. You need to document it by sending a picture to the owner. The owner has ultimate decision as to whether you should take the dog to the vet, or apply any medication or treatment by yourself.

I always have Children's Benadryl available. I also have anti-diarrhea medicine tablets, antacids, and things like that.

You really want to be careful about diarrhea. That can create a really difficult situation. Be careful with the treats, go light. If you see a loose stool in the yard, that probably means you are giving too many treats or too rich treats.

Don't let dogs dig near the fence perimeter. I think you should place one foot square paving stones along the entire inside perimeter of your fenced yard. The reason is, dogs can dig under anything else that you would put there. They cannot dig past a big brick.

I also use bricks to plug up any dog holes that were dug in the center of the yard. I used to use sand, fill dirt, and nothing works better than a big heavy brick. I used to even put dog poop in the holes but they would still dig. I really don't care too much about the dogs digging in the center of the yard, but around the perimeter that's a No-No.

You cannot put anything that is tall near the fence perimeter. Dogs are very acrobatic and they can easily jump off a small milk crate, or AC unit, and get over the fence.

I inspect my fence and yard every single day. I need to be aware of the condition of the fence and everything else in the yard. I have to search for mushrooms growing, poisonous plants, and I also inspect the condition of the poop to make sure the dogs are healthy.

Don't allow dogs to eat poop. That is a bad thing.

I think for the most part the only difficult dog I'm not willing to deal with is the aggressive dog. It's just too much headache and it's not fair to the other dogs to live in fear of an aggressive dog. But a sick dog, a neurotic dog, an old dog, or a blind dog, I'm totally fine with those dogs.

I'm not a big fan of destructive dogs. Your dog beds are vulnerable to attack. If a dog rips up my dog bed, that dog will be put in the exercise pen with no dog bed.

You should wrap your dog beds in heavy duty contractor trash bags, the largest you can find. This way, the dog will destroy the trash bag, and not the actual bed inside. The trash bag is also great for stopping pee and poop from touching the dog bed.

I love fitted sheets, because they wrap around a dog bed so well. If you use an unfitted sheet it will shift and move and expose the bed underneath and that's not good.

Sometimes dogs will come to your home in a very stressed out state. They will have separation anxiety, and they will be confused as to why their owner dropped them off at this strange place, with these strange dogs.

You need to be aware of a stressed out dog. If she is foaming and drooling, she's stressed out. If she's not eating, she's stressed out. In those situations, your best bet is to isolate the dog.

I have a back room, I call it the French Room, because it has clear glass french doors. When I put a dog in that room by herself, she can still see the other dogs through the glass door, but she cannot be threatened by them, or threaten the others. So I use this method to slowly let the dog get comfortable with the other dogs.

When a dog first comes into my home, having never been here before, I will introduce the dog and I will have a dish rag in my hand. If any dog is intrusive aggressive or showing bully behavior, I will warn them with a loud voice, and if that's not enough I will take the dish rag and give him a little pop.

I cannot allow any dogs to feel threatened, picked on, or unsafe. Any dog unable to get along with others is going to be quarantined until the end of the stay, and then most likely that dog will not be welcome to return.

Part of security is keeping your home safe for clients to access. In winter months I have to use ice-melt to keep my driveway ice free and the ramp in the backyard. I built a ramp with wooden steps on it, that goes from the doggie door to the fenced yard, a slope of about 3 feet. The reason I made the ramp is because steps are too difficult for puppies and old dogs. The ramp is the easiest possible entry in and out of the doggie door.

In my home, I do not like to have clear glass windows. The reason is, I don't want the dogs to peek out the windows, looking for their owners. However, I do love natural sunlight. So I winterize my windows, both with one-way window tint which allows the sunlight in, and on other windows I put clear plastic wrap on the windows, which will allow the sunlight in, but no one can see in or out.

If you allow a dog access to a window that overlooks the street, the dogs will ruin your drapes and curtains, and bark at everything that passes by. You should cover the window, even if you have to put plywood up, because the dogs won't give you any rest. They will constantly be peeking out the window, waiting for their owner to return.

I can't think of much else to say about difficult dogs. My goal is to have a home full of well-behaved dogs, who are regular guests and familiar with my home routine. I do some unofficial training when the dog is here with me on a vacation stay, because I want the dog to feel accepted and in harmony with our schedule and our home life.

Some dogs, like the Mastiff or the English Bulldog, they drool constantly. You will need to carry a drool rag, and change the water bowl frequently.

I feel like difficult dogs are part of the business, but there's a certain level of difficulty on safety that I'm not willing to budge on. If a dog is unsafe, I don't want that dog in my home. But if a dog is simply difficult, I can handle that.

Let's talk about difficult owners.

Some owners will expect ridiculous things from you. A few owners are irresponsible people and should not own a dog. 99% of owners are wonderful people and I believe that dog owners are the best people in the world. But there are a few owners that are just bad people and in this business, like any other business, you will eventually meet a bad person.

If you get a difficult client, practice good judgment. If you feel this person is so difficult that you don't want to do business with him, you should just text him and tell him that this is not a good fit, and that's the end of that. Any rude client, as long as they don't owe me money, I will usually say good luck and goodbye, and block them from my phone.

Difficult clients exist and for that reason I personally don't have my reviews turned on my Facebook page. I used to be really proud of my reviews, and then I got a lady who was upset about something, and she gave me a real ugly review, and I felt like turning off the review so that could not happen again. So I literally had one bad review and I decided I didn't want to be graded that way. Use your own judgment in that regard. I feel like a review is super important when you're a new business, so I recommend turning your reviews on, on your new Facebook page. But if it ever becomes a problem you can always turn it off again.

On Facebook I hold all comments for review. Again, I haven't had much of a problem with trolls or rude people, but I want to manage my page in case a difficult client tries to smear me.

I do my utmost to make every client feel special and make their stay enjoyable. Just like any business, no one gets 100% customer satisfaction. But that is my goal. When a client is unhappy, it's very easy in our business to simply finish the training or finish the stay, and then put an asterisk by their name in your phone, so the next time they call you can politely decline to do business.

I think in the last six or seven years, I had 2 clients who paid me with either bad checks or with bad promises to pay. One time I threatened to file a complaint with the police and the client paid. The other time the client offered to give me a fraction of what was owed, claiming that's all he had. I don't accept credit card payments but I do accept check and cash and PayPal.

Sometimes I will get a client who is retired or has a lot of time on her hands, and she will want to talk and text a whole lot. I have to pace myself on those conversations, because I can't be distracted from doing my job with the dogs.

Difficult clients are a lot like difficult dogs. You will be able to work with most difficult people, and figure out a way to get the job done. But there is a boundary at which a difficult dog and a difficult client become more than you're willing to deal with. And then you can decide not to do business with them.

I have strong marketing. And what that means is, if I decline to take a pit bull, if I say no to an aggressive German Shepherd, if I decline to watch a bull mastiff/wolf hybrid, I am okay with that decision. Because I know that tomorrow, an owner of a Maltese cute little puppy is going to call me. If I accept the Wolf Mastiff, I will have to decline The Maltese pup. So I want my home to be filled with gentle friendly mellow dogs. They can be hyper, and they can play all they want in the yard, and chase each other, without being bullies or rough play, but when it's night time they got to be quiet and let me sleep.

Sometimes people are weird, and in this business you're going to see more than one weird person. But again, for the most part I love my clients Every one of them is a great person, and they love dogs, and so we have that common bond. I love my clients and in 7 years of doing this I can only think of two clients that were very unpleasant.

ᘓ(ˉ .ェ ˉ)ʋ

Busy Weekends & Holidays

Most of my dog sitting business is on weekends and holidays.

This is frustrating because I would prefer a more even distribution of clients throughout the year. But instead the way it works is, I am super busy on Labor Day, Thanksgiving and Christmas, and spring break, and then slowest in the winter months.

On a busy weekend, I have to be on top of the house cleaning, the monitoring of the dogs, the feedings, and the walks.

I usually have a limit of 10 to 13 dogs. When things get this busy I will make a separate list on a clipboard to keep track of all the dogs.

I never have time to do a meet-and-greet, or therapy dog visits, or running errands and such. On a busy weekend or a holiday, I have to stay home and be with the dogs. It would be irresponsible to leave that many dogs unsupervised.

If you are lucky enough to have a wife or family member who can give you a break once in a while during the busy days, that is a big help. I have yet to find someone who can be trusted to sit in my home with the dogs and who would be interested in such a minor part time work.

I would never put any advertisements up during the busy weekends, because I know I will be full capacity on holidays and busy weekends. Instead, I try to market towards regular clients, like puppy training and doggy day care and therapy dog visits. This will balance my schedule more evenly throughout the year, instead of having too many dogs on holidays, and not enough dogs in the winter.

One holiday I want to talk about is 4th of July. Another is January 1st. Both of these holidays are likely to have fireworks and even guns being shot in the nighttime. You are likely to have at least one dog who is thunder shy, and already stressed out, because she is away from home, and the safety of her owners. How should you deal with this panic-stricken dog?

Again, you have to be physically present with this many dogs. I recommend sitting in front of a television and stroking the stressed-out dog. Hold the dog firmly so she can't do anything harmful, and your presence should help her feel better.

When major holidays approach, my priority is to have my house full of dogs that I already know and trust to behave well. So I usually message my regular clients and ask them if they need a sitter for the holiday. The reason I do this is because if I book new clients first, and then my regulars ask me for the same dates, it is very hard to say no to my regular clients, because I could lose their business. A regular client is worth twice as much financially as a seasonal vacation client. This is a rough estimate but I feel it's true. If a lady brings me her dog two or three times a week for doggie daycare, that adds up to more than a week-long vacation once a year. So my regular clients are very special, because I get to know them better and I get to know their dogs very well.

If anyone calls you after you are fully booked and cannot accept any more dogs, you can choose to refer them to Rover.com. I feel my priority is finding the dogs a place that is safe. Rover is a great service.

I do not charge any extra fee for holidays but Rover does charge a modest amount, I think 10%.

When I have a house at full capacity, I am careful not to take photos of a crowded house. No videos either. Even though I don't feel that many dogs is unreasonable, I don't want to present a public image of so many dogs. So for that reason, no more than two or three dogs in a picture.

If your clients are traveling out of the country, it may be hard for them to receive your text messages and updates about the dog. They probably have Facebook Messenger and it would be easier to send pictures to their Messenger account while they are gone.

ᕫ(˘ ˳ ˘)ʊ

Keeping A Daily Schedule

I have a clipboard that never leaves my sight. On this clipboard I write down every upcoming stay with a dog. I know the arrival day, both the date and day of the week, the dog's name, and the departure date. I may also make small notes regarding special offers, or a note about the breed of the dog.

If an appointment is more than two months out, I put those appointments on a long-term list which I check once a month and that list goes in the very back of my clipboard. So if it's July and someone wants to reserve a stay for Christmas, I will write that reservation on the very last page of my clipboard.

I have a top sheet of my clipboard which is the day's events. It will show every dog who is coming and going, along with certain important errands and tasks that I need to get done. This is my outline for the day. It is my "to do" list.

Many times when you are dealing with people on vacation, they are traveling long distances, and they are getting on and off planes, so when they tell you they're coming at 2 it could be between 2 and 3. So I write on my list "2ish" if it is a rough estimate of time.

I like to schedule meet-and-greets when everything is nice and calm, and that is in the center of the day. Mornings are busy because of drop offs, dog walks, and feeding. Evenings are busy because of dogs being picked up, feeding, and honestly it's time to relax a bit in the evening.

Once an owner does the meet-and-greet for the first time and sees the home and everything, after that point we never venture deeper into the home than the laundry room. There is no need for the owner to go deep inside the home and excite the dogs. It is very hard to talk to an owner, with all the distractions that a pack of dogs could bring. So when the owner comes to pick up her dog, I have the leash on the dog and I walk that single dog outside. This makes for a calm, smooth transition.

I have tried many of those digital day planners and schedulers. There are 100 apps that offer great day planners, but for this business I just never found one that was easier than handwriting on a blank piece of paper for my schedule and my reservation list. Perhaps I'm just not willing to adapt. You should do whatever works for you.

One tip I will share with you: If a client wants to book a stay 6 months in advance, you can send a gmail to yourself, with the stay information, and schedule the email to deliver the message 5 months from now, when it becomes important.

ᘛ(˘ ⚬ ˘)ᘚ

Barking

I do not allow barking in my home. I train puppies, so if even one dog barks, the puppy will learn that behavior, and its owner will not be happy. I believe that barking is a mini aggression, and for that reason I do not allow it. A single barking dog at night can keep the entire home awake.

Usually a dog will be in the fenced yard, and she will see someone walk by on the sidewalk, it could be a child or another dog walking, and she will bark. I will go outside and tell her "No barking!" If she does it again, she's going inside for a timeout in the exercise pen for 5 to 15 minutes.

Barking is not a difficult habit to break in my opinion. I have a bark collar but I never use it. It's weird because owners will tell me that the dog barks all the time at their home, but when I'm alone with the dog and I say "No barking!" I don't get a lot of resistance from the dogs.

One form of barking is the whining that a puppy will do in the crate at night when they first arrived at my home. This will also keep everyone awake all night if allowed. Usually this is how I solve the problem. I will first shout at the puppy "No!" And I will use my squirt bottle of water to squirt the puppy and encourage her to stop.

If that doesn't work, I will take a dish rag, while the puppy is in the crate, and I will whack the crate fiercely with the dish rag. I want to over-dramatize my anger so the dog reads my body language and my emotion.

The truth is I cannot hurt the dog because the dog is in the crate, but she doesn't know that. So she thinks that I go crazy whenever I hear whining. Usually the whining will stop the first night, but definitely by the second night. If it is a rough first night for you, I used to call it Hell Night, another technique I do is I put the crate with the whining puppy in the bathroom. This will muffle the sound so that you can get some sleep.

If you are trying to solve the problem of barking, there are plenty of great bark collars. These devices are worn on the neck and they admit a little zap whenever the sensor feels the throat grumbling. I don't use them because I never have a need, but I do have bark collars, and I would use them if nothing else worked. But for me personally all I do is insist on no barking, and I give them a time out if they are slow to figure it out.

6(ﬞ· ⚡ ﬞ·)ʊ

Meet & Greet

A meet-and-greet is when a prospective client wants to do business with you, but she want to meet you first, and see your home, and get a feel for your professionalism. She is trusting you with her dog, her little baby, and she wants to feel good knowing the dog is safe and cared for.

When you schedule the meet-and-greet, do it in the slowest part of your day. Usually around noon or 1 pm. You may have to work around their schedule.

You should never schedule a meet-and-greet on a super busy holiday or weekend. This will not impress a prospect, and it's not safe to be distracted, with a house full of dogs. Schedule it at a slower time.

I always scrub my house good before a meet-and-greet. If I have a terribly disruptive dog in my home, I will put that dog in the exercise pen, while the prospect is here. I don't want that dog to make me look bad.

Most times the prospect will bring her dog, and I will meet the dog, usually outside at first. I usually will reach down and pet the dog. If you think a dog might possibly nip at you, you always want to make your hand a fist, because it's harder to bite around a fist, than individual, spread-open fingers.

After we have established rapport, and the dog is friendly, I will silently take the leash from the owner. I do this because I need to see how the dog responds to me handling her. I also want the owner to trust me handling her dog.

If they have been driving a distance, I will invite the dog to pee or poop on the front yard.

I am silently assessing the dog's behavior while talking to the owner, and then we will naturally proceed inside the home. I go through the laundry room and into the kitchen, where the barn door separates the kitchen from the living room.

I have no intention of letting the new dog meet my group of dogs during the meet-and-greet.

What I will do is, I'll put a baby gate at the front of the barn door, and open the barn door slightly, so the owner can look in my living room and see the dogs looking back at her, friendly and curious.

Then I can show her the backyard, by going outside in the back. It is not safe to introduce her dog to my group of dogs while the owner is here.

Sometimes, you will meet a dog that is not a good fit for your business. If a dog has serious health issues that you don't feel comfortable handling, you should decline the stay. If the dog is so fearful that she is nipping, trembling, frightened, and you don't feel comfortable, you can recommend a different sitter.

Most of the things I say to the owner at a meet-and-greet is very patterned phrases that I have practiced saying for years.

When a dog is at my door, and I'm holding the leash, sometimes the dog will resist coming into the home. It looks horrible if I were to try to drag the dog by the leash into the home. I am a man, so I like to gently pick up the dog and bring the dog inside. This tells the dog silently that I will gently force him to do what I need him to do. It also silently tells the owner that I can handle the dog if I have to.

To be honest, I sometimes discourage meet-and-greets. I say something like this, "If you are busy, and don't have time for a meet-and-greet, you can visit my Facebook or YouTube page, I have posted over 500 videos of me working with dogs, and videos of my home, and the dogs that are there."

I feel like if they can't get a good feeling from the videos, they're not going to get much more by visiting my home. But if they still need a meet-and-greet, I am happy to do one, as long as it is during a slow part of the day, not on a busy weekend or holiday.

ᕦ(͡° ͜ʖ ͡°)ᕤ

Poop

Let's talk about the world of dog poop. Picking up poop and pee is 20% of your job. Doing it right is going to save you a ton of frustration and headache.

When you get up in the morning, the first thing you do is take all the dogs outside to go pee. I usually use the baby gate to keep the dogs from running back inside. After I let them outside to go pee, I will go back upstairs and put my clothes on. If I did this in reverse, putting my clothes on first, the dogs would hear me upstairs, they would wake up, and the puppies would probably have an accident.

I also give the dogs a midnight pee break. This is important when you are training puppies. If you don't do this midnight pee break, the pup might pee in the crate.

I have to pick up dog poop every single day in my backyard. But I imagine every dog owner, everywhere, has to pick up poop, because it doesn't magically pick itself up, and dogs don't know how to use a toilet. So every dog owner is picking up poop, but I pick up just a little bit more.

I can never get behind on my poop pickup. If I do, the dogs will step in the poop and track it in the house. And because the poop on their paws is a small amount, it may take me awhile to find where the phantom smells are coming from. I may have to scrub everything.

I have a poop bucket outside, it is a 5-gallon bucket with a plastic lid on it. I don't close the lid completely, because it's difficult to open, instead I pinch it closed in two spots. This is sufficient to keep dogs out of it and make it easy for me to open. By the way, I also use these 5 gallon buckets with lids as trash cans in dog areas. The lids are ideal because the dogs can't get inside the bucket. The bucket I have in the living room is a twist lid Gamma style and I really like it.

So my method for cleaning poop in the yard is a take a poop bag, and put it on my hand like a glove. I grab my poop bucket by the handle with the lid already off. Then I proceed to scan the yard in a row-by-row fashion, picking up any poop I see, as well as anything else that seems unsafe for the dogs. That could be old toys that have fallen apart, tree branches that have fallen into the yard, mushrooms, old pieces of plastic, anything that a dog should not be chewing.

When the bucket is full, I dump it into a standard kitchen size trash bag, tie it up and put it beside the trash cans.

I buy my poop bags at the Meijer, I buy them 20 rolls at a time. Because this is my business, and my neighbors are usually watching me, I can never ever leave a poop on my walk without picking it up. This is bad for business.

And it's just plain unsanitary. Another reason why I pick up all my poop is because I walk the same route every day, so if I leave a poop today, it will be there tomorrow, and the next day.

I have to have more than enough poop bags, so that I never get caught without one. To solve this problem, I devised a system. I fill my two back pockets with 10 poop bags each. Then I use the poop bags in my right pocket first. As soon as the poop bags in my right pocket are empty, I put one poop bag in my front pocket, to remind me to refill my bags.

I also have spare poop bags in my jacket pocket and my wallet. I have spare poop bags in my car as well. I should never run out of poop bags it's just not good for a dog sitter to do that.

When you pick up a dog's poop, now you have a big bag of poop in your hand, and you are thinking of the nearest trash can. Sometimes a trash can is not nearby. I feel like it can be a safety hazard to have one hand full of poop while you are managing multiple dogs on a leash. In situations like this I may decide to put the bag of poop on the side of the sidewalk, where I can clearly see it. Then when I circle back around and return home, I will walk the same way, pick up the poop and return home.

I have no problem putting my dog poop in some neighbors trash can.

There will be times when you simply cannot pick up a dog's poop.

If you walk the dog at night time, or early morning, you may not be able to see the poop. If it's raining hard or snowing hard, you may not be able to see the poop. Sometimes a dog will poop in a pile of autumn leaves and the camouflage will be perfect and you will not see the poop. I've had other dogs poop right in the middle of the crosswalk in a busy intersection, and I felt it was unsafe to attempt to clean the poop right there. Use your best judgment. Your goal is to be safe and be clean. If you can only be one of those things, be safe.

If you get poop on your hand, look for a grass or a green leaf outside to clean the poop off your fingers. I would rub my fingers in the dirt if I could not get to a hose or bathroom.

If you get poop on your shoes, the best thing to do is look for a small twig

that is sturdy and firm. I will use the twig to trace the grooves in my shoe
and flick the poop off my sole. Then with most of the big pieces of poop out
of the way I will polish the shoe sole in grass or in snow for a final clean.

You can tell a lot from a dog's behavior by his poop. Sometimes a dog will
be stressed out from separation anxiety and the dog will be a little homesick.
This will cause a diarrhea or loose stool. Other times loose stool is caused by
chewing rocks or twigs, eating a new brand of dog food or treats that upset
the stomach, things like that.

When you see loose stool in the yard, it's important for you to identify who's
poop it is. How big is the poop? If it's a certain size, it has to come from a
certain size dog. You want to find out which dog made the runny poop, so
you can monitor that dog's diet and behavior closely.

Things you should never see in poop include pieces of plastic, pieces of
rope. You will definitely see grass in dog poop, because dogs eat grass as a
sort of natural antacid to deal with upset stomach. When you see grass in the
dog's poop, that will tell you that the dog recently had indigestion, and ate the
grass to calm her stomach and flush out impurities.

As a dog sitter, your nose will be trained to smell poop and pee instantly, at at
the tiniest amounts. I can smell a small puppies pee from the next room, and
I can smell dog poop from upstairs when it happens downstairs.

When a dog poops in my home, I will isolate the poop accident, by removing
the dogs from that area.

I use empty grocery plastic bags for indoor poop pick up. I will scoop up all
the solid matter in the grocery bag, and take it outside to the trash area where
I have a 5 gallon bucket waiting. This bucket has no lid, because in these
types of emergencies I want to throw the poop in there quickly, and come
back to finish cleaning the house. Once I return, I will pour some Lysol on
the area, ring my mop and mop the area clean. I will find the offending dog,
scold her and put her in a time out.

If you have a natural disgust for poop, you should desensitize yourself to it
now, so you can be an effective dog sitter. Everybody poops, and dogs poop
too. You just pick up the poop everyday, and eventually it becomes no big
deal.

Do you want to know an easy way to make extra money? When I was a new dog sitter, I would charge people $50 to clean the poop from their yard, after the winter thaw. It was easy work. I would go out and usually knock out a yard in 20 minutes. It was also a great way to talk to dog owners in my area and offer them dog sitting services.

If you give a dog some weird stuff to eat, you will probably be dealing with diarrhea, the most dreaded form of poop. When we talk about diarrhea, two things are super important to remember.

If you see any blood in the stool, that's a problem and a visit to the veterinarian is probably mandated.

The next thing about diarrhea you need to remember is that you don't want to confine a dog, who has diarrhea, to a very small space. If you keep a puppy in a crate and she has diarrhea, she's going to have an accident, and then step in it, and lay in it, and then she's going to hate herself because she stinks, and she's covered in poop, and she's going to start whining, pawing at the crate wires, covering them in poop. When you finally find her you're going to have to wash the puppy and the entire crate by hand.

What you want to do if a dog has diarrhea, is keep her in enough space so that she can have an accident, and then sleep in a different area. You want to keep this dog away from other dogs.

What do you give the dog to solve the diarrhea problem? Well if the dog is on her normal kibble, and you didn't change the kibble recently, I recommend her normal kibble, mixed with a little chicken and rice.

If the diarrhea is really bad, I can give the dogs a small Pepto-Bismol tablet or antacid tablet mixed in peanut butter. You should never give any medication to a dog without the owner's approval first.

If a dog suddenly gets diarrhea, I will usually take a picture of it and share it with the owner. It is their responsibility to tell me whether I should wait and see if it goes away or if I should take the dog to a vet visit. I do not charge extra for vet visits. It's just part of the job, a service I offer.

When you're giving dogs treats you should stick to treats that are gentle on the stomach. Some treats may taste wonderful, but you will see loose stool later, and those treats are not ideal.

I do not pay for most of my dog treats. When a client asks me what they should bring with their dog, for either training or a vacation stay, I recommend they bring dog food and any treats. So I have a ton of treats in the home.

If I have treats that are not popular with the dogs or treats that upset their stomach, I will toss them.

If you are trying to clean your yard and it is bad weather and snowy, what I like to do is I take my shovel and I dig around the poop and toss the poop around the perimeter of the fence. This way dogs are not stepping in poop in the middle of the yard. Dogs will not usually walk around the extreme edge of the fence. I throw all the poop towards the edge of the fence, and then when the snow melts I will pick up the poop easily in a straight line along the fence.

The dog beds all have a thick contractor trash bag covering them, and a fitted bed sheet. So if the dog poops or pees on the dog beds, I replace the fitted sheet, I spray down the trash bag with Lysol and wipe it down and with the fitted sheet replaced we are all set.

I have taught my personal dogs the command, "Go outside?" I say it like a question and if they need to go outside they will stand near the door.

I train the puppies to understand the "Go Pee" command. Every time they go poo or pee, I calmly say, "good girl, go pee." This becomes a command they understand and associate with pee or poop.

I have a hamper in the back room, with an airtight locking lid. This hamper is where I put dirty towels and rags that may have poop or pee on them. I wash them separately, and I'm careful not to use harsh detergents, because dogs have sensitive skin when it comes to soaps.

You should always have Febreze available to help your house recover from an indoor poop.

Ⳙ(⁻ ⋅ ⁻)ʊ

Security

Security is everything in the dog business. Let's break this down in to Safety Issues, and General Security Issues.

Safety is everything. I do not allow any rough play in my home. Dogs have to play nice. They can't be chewing on things, because that is not safe.

I have pillows shoved behind the couch and under furniture, so small dogs cannot crawl underneath things and hide. I have blocked off access to any extension cords or hidden wires. I don't want any puppies chewing on any wires. For my own personal computer in the living room, I have created a sheath of hard durable plastic tubing and I put all my electrical cords in the sheath. This will prevent any dog from nibbling on the wires.

I make sure that no wires are dangling from behind appliances. Rather than turn on one light at a time in my living room, I have all six of my lights on a master remote switch. This helps me illuminate the entire room quickly.

I have a huge barn door that separates the kitchen from the living room area where the dogs live. The barn door security is important. If any dog goes sniffing or digging near the door I will put them in a time out.

If I see any digging near the perimeter of the fence, I will put a brick there to stop the digging. These bricks weigh 15 lb and they are roughly a foot square.

When I'm walking the dogs, I usually use a prong collar if I see any pulling at all. I want the dog to respect me during the walk, which is the most vulnerable time for escapes.

When I'm going to leave the house for an errand or to walk the dogs, I will look at my group of dogs, and if I don't feel like a certain dog can be trusted alone while I'm out, that dog will go in the exercise pen, or a crate, or if the weather is nice I would just put them outside. But they have to make me feel like I can trust them. Usually that's not a problem. Right now I have 10 dogs in the home and I trust them all, enough for me to go to the gym or to the grocery store for an hour.

I don't like to bring new clients into my dog area, because that is a security

risk. They might forget to close the barn door, or they might let a dog slip
out from behind them. Dogs are clever escape artists, and an absent-minded
owner is common.

I have three remote security cameras, that video stream my living room, my
dog room, and my backyard. So if I'm at the grocery store, I can look on my
cell phone app, and see any part of the dog areas. What's even cooler is, I can
actually speak through the audio of my phone, and the dogs will hear me. I
can also hear them, but they don't say much, LOL.

I never use my front door. I feel it's too risky for dogs to run outside. I
believe in vestibule design, where there are two doors, like an airlock for a
spaceship. If by some freak accident the dog gets past the first door, he
cannot get past the second door.

When the weather is bad, excessively rainy or extremely cold snowy weather,
I will close the doggie door. I feel it is better to risk a poop or pee accident in
the home, than to see a dog freezing or soaked outside in a storm. During
these times I usually look for a break in the weather, to give them their much-
needed potty breaks.

When someone rings my doorbell, which by the way is a "Ring" doorbell, the
electronic kind that lets me see who is at my door, through my smartphone, I
do not open the front door. Instead I go around through the back door and
meet them in the front.

I have a gate in the backyard that is a service gate. This gate is also a
vestibule system, consisting of two separate gates. Just like you would see
two gates at the dog park. The dog park would be a bad idea if it just had one
gate, and dogs could slip in and out easily.

A big part of security is for me to adopt an attitude of complete confidence
and control of the environment. Act as if everything is normal and under
control and the dogs (and the clients) will pick up on that feeling and relax.
Any trouble maker dogs, or dogs panicking from separation anxiety, will be
given their own space, and encouraged to fit in with the pack.

There are three or four dogs that come to my home that are exceptionally well
behaved. I am talking about off-leash dogs. I take these dogs to the meadow
and let them run free regularly. So this privilege is not extended to 95% of

the dogs in my home. I have taught these off-leash dogs special commands that keep them within my visual sight and within the range of my voice. You can train your dogs to be off-leash dogs but again, they have to be exceptionally smart and obedient, and it will take months for you to have a reliable off leash dog.

One safety issue is ice and snow. You have to have ice-melt. They sell the snow melt that is paw friendly but personally I don't think it does a good job. Use whatever feels right to you. I usually buy what is available when I need it and although I prefer the salt, either one will work.

If you have frozen parts of your driveway, your customers can easily slip-on the ice because the dogs are excited and pulling on the leash. First, you can use the ice-melt salt. I also have a chipping tool that will allow you to break up stubborn ice, and if that doesn't work a propane torch will get any tough spots to melt.

One thing that helps me in my city, is that we have very low crime. If you live in a high-crime area, you can't do the same things I do. I remember when I lived near Detroit, people would actually steal dogs, and then wait for the ransom. If you live in a high-crime area, you will need automatic security lights, maybe even some barbed wire and some Compton steel bars on your windows. I don't pretend to know much about your local area, but you do have to feel safe in your home, like no one can easily go in there and mess with your dogs.

My fenced yard has two outer gates and they are both locked with a combination lock. The side door of my home is the main entrance for dog customers and it is usually locked. The sliding glass door in the kitchen is locked. The front door is locked and never opened. Both my porch light and my patio light go on automatically upon sensing motion.

I wasn't happy with the view of the dogs and the people who walk by my home on the sidewalk. Sometimes they are walking dogs, or children, and that would make my dogs want to bark. So I put up a black tarp on the fence that allows some light in, but obscures the view just enough so the dogs don't bark.

I am always looking for small gaps along the base of the fence line. I am constantly putting bricks there, and using wire and grates to shut off any possible escape routes.

If a new client is coming to my home, I will politely text them and ask them to use the side door, and to message me when they arrive, so that the doorbell does not disturb the dogs. In this way I'm training the client to message me when they arrive because the dogs really do get excited when someone rings the doorbell.

ᕦ(ˉ ꒳ ˉ)ᕤ

Paperwork

I think you would be surprised to know that I don't have any forms or contracts or paperwork that I share with my clients.

The reason why is because I don't want to make myself vulnerable to lawsuits. In this business, it is possible for a dog to get sick, injured or even die while in my care. I do everything I can to see that the dogs are safe and healthy, but just as in real life, accidents happen, and I don't want to be sued for an accident.

Let's pretend that a dog comes to my home and gets bit by another dog. This is possible even though I will do everything to prevent it. If you think this is not possible then you are not ready to be in the dog business. Even dog groomers have to deal with aggressive dogs and just like the groomers, I don't give any formal paperwork to my clients regarding their rights and what they can expect.

If a dog gets bit in my home, the owner would likely be upset. If she goes to a lawyer, the lawyer will ask her what paperwork she received from me. He is going to go over that paperwork, looking for any way to sue me, for as much as he can.

So if I give the client no paperwork at all, then she has no contractual agreement with me.

If I get a client who asks too many questions about rights and responsibilities and all of that, I just politely decline to watch their dog. This does not hurt my business at all. I know that as soon as I hang up the phone with this person, another nice lady will call me and she will not mention paperwork at all.

There is another disadvantage with providing your clients with forms and paperwork. That takes time from your other responsibilities, like watching the dogs, walking the dogs, and spending time with them.

So if you want my sage advice, I would not have any contracts at all. Not for dog training and not for dog sitting. The only exception to that is Rover.com. Of course they will have an online agreement with the client and with you.

As a sitter for Rover.com, you should definitely be familiar with the terms of your contract. For example, I can tell you that although Rover offers insurance for their stays, the insurance does not cover much, and it was written by a lawyer who definitely works to protect Rover's interests, and not yours.

The only paperwork I do for my clients is graduation paperwork, for puppy training or for therapy dogs. With the therapy dogs, I like to use a local trophy shop, and make a beautiful Rose Wood plaque, with the dogs picture sealed in clear plastic, and below that it says the dog's name and "Certified Therapy Dog" in bold, with the year. This makes for an impressive memento of the dogs training.

For puppy training, I prepare a graduation folder. This folder has a blue Canine Good Citizen ribbon on the front. Inside, there is a two-page progress report, that covers every single part of the dog's training. I give the new owner practical advice, on how to keep the dog learning and growing and behaving well. This advice includes walking the dog daily, practicing the basic commands every day, installing a doggy door, and how to correct a dog when she makes a mistake. The last part of the graduation folder is the AKC form for Canine Good Citizen or CGC. This form is filled out by me, and then mailed by the client to AKC for the official certificate.

You do not need a business license to do dog sitting or dog training. At least not in my state. If you live in America you probably do not need a business license.

What you do on tax day is your business. I am not here to tell you how much to pay or what to declare. I will say that most of the income from the dog business is cash. So you have some flexibility on what you declare to the government. Because you are a home-based business, you don't need a business license, because you don't sell a product or service that requires government oversight, and you are not leasing a retail space to sell products to the public. You are responsible for your taxes, but you will most likely declare your income on a standard 1040 with no deductions.

I do not like to promote my dog business at my actual location. That is because I don't like government scrutiny. There are limits in my neighborhood as to how many dogs a private owner can have. Technically, the local authorities could limit my business, and so I don't want to do any direct advertising from my front yard.

When a client comes to my home, sometimes they will want to prepay for the service. If someone hands me money, I want to give them a receipt quickly. The easiest way to do that, is to send that person a text message, saying, "I received $250 from you today for watching your dog. Thank you for the business!" No paper trail.

The Genius of giving a text message as a receipt is that the owner does not have a physical receipt in their hand, but you have a record of any prepayments they may have made, because you would just check your text messages for that client.

If someone were to ask me for my credentials as a dog trainer or dog sitter, I would point them to the hundreds and hundreds of videos I have posted on Facebook and YouTube. These videos show my expertise more than any diploma or certificate. Anyone who asks you for more proof of your qualifications is an idiot and you should decline to do business with them.

I am an AKC certified trainer, so I have proof of that. When you walk into my home, I have my AKC certificate framed on the wall, next to other impressive diplomas, and a newspaper article about how I help re-home stray dogs.

By now you are getting a impression, for how I feel about paperwork. If a prospective client bugs me for paperwork, I will blow off the request and if they continue, I will decline to work with them. I do this because I know I don't need to prove anything to anyone. My reputation and skill is not something I care to prove to anyone. Word of mouth and strong media presence will bring new clients to my door, and I don't have time or inclination to be running around showing people my certificates and diplomas.

I have never been sued by a lawyer, not even a close call. Trust me if you've been doing this as long as I have, problems arise, and when they do, your strength will be that you had no written contract with the clients, so their legal options are very limited. They have the same legal rights as if they asked the neighbor to watch their dog.

I am not trying to avoid responsibility for the dogs. I love dogs and that's why I'm in this business, and I do everything to keep them safe and comfortable. But the reality of living on planet Earth is that sometimes accidents happen. Sometimes dogs bite each other. Sometimes a dog is sick and old and may die in your care. In any of those situations, I don't want some crooked lawyer scrutinizing any written contract for loopholes where they can prosecute me. No contract means I have a big advantage in the court.

One last thing about paperwork. If you plan to join Rover.com, you will be required to pass a background check. And if you decide to become an AKC evaluator, they will require two years of proof that you work with dogs. This requirement is easy to fulfill. Simply start a Facebook page, and call it a dog sitting business. Once you start this page, and put a few dog pictures, you will have proof that you are in the dog business. You need to be in the dog business two years before you can become an AKC evaluator. So my advice is to put down this book right now, and start your new Facebook page today. Then exactly two years from today, you will qualify to be an AKC evaluator.

ʕ(¯·ᴥ·¯)ʋ

Sick Dogs

Let's talk about sick dogs for a moment.

There are some illnesses that you don't want a dog to bring into your home. The worst one is parvo. If you hear of any dogs having parvo or contact with parvo they cannot come to your home for any reason.

Parvo is extremely contagious and it kills puppies fast. The vaccine for parvo is usually not given until the dog is a certain age, so the puppies are vulnerable. Parvo kills so fast you won't even have time to recognize the symptoms.

Sometimes a litter of puppies will have an outbreak of Parvo, and some of the puppies will survive. You cannot let those puppies in your home, because they are carriers for the disease. Parvo is horrible, in that it lives in the grass and it can stay there for a years. It will ruin your business, so you cannot ever allow a parvo dog in your home.

Rabies shots or normal and part of every vaccination treatment. I've been doing this job for 7 years and I've never met a dog that had rabies. I think the disease might have been common at one point but now it's very rare.

Many times an owner will ask me if it's okay that his dog is not up to date on shots. I'm not too worried about rabies. But parvo is important and also I want them to get their shots for kennel cough. I want the dogs to be healthy, so I kind of push the owner to get the shots before the dog comes to me.

Obviously, an 8 week young puppy does not have her full battery of shots. But she has her first set of shots so that is good. I have not had a puppy related illness in 7 years.

I would be very careful letting any dog with a contagious illness in the home. I wouldn't want a dog in my home that had fleas or ticks. I have been very lucky about fleas and ticks in that I have not had any.

Dogs get sick and dogs get old. I love all dogs, and I believe in giving comfort and care to the sick and old dogs. So even if a dog is unable to control her pee or poo, or needs help going inside and outside, or need special bathing or medication, I am willing to help the dog in this way.

If a dog requires special trips to the veterinarian, or special trip to the groomer, I charge a fee for that.

A dog has never died in my home, but it is entirely possible that it could happen one day.

Let's suppose a dog is healthy in my home, and then I notice a scratch, or a rash, or an irritated eye, or maybe I notice the dog is chewing on her tail excessively, or maybe she just threw up, or she just did a diarrhea poop. For any of these conditions, I will immediately photograph the injury or illness, I will write a description of what I see and I will text that to the owner and ask for their advice and opinion.

If the owner wants me to take the dog to the veterinarian I will do so promptly. Of course they will have to work out the billing arrangement with the veterinarian. I do not cover the veterinarian bills. That is never a part of this business.

Usually we will solve the problem together. The owner may have seen the problem before and if so, she will know exactly what to do. For example if I see a rash on the hind legs perhaps the owner will say the dog is allergic to something and to give her a Benadryl. Or if the dog gets diarrhea the owner may say it's because of her medication. The owner is ultimately responsible for the dog but I am responsible for notifying the owner of any change in health.

A dog who is sick should be kept close enough so you can watch her. If a dog has diarrhea, I don't want that dog to be crated. The dog should be put in a small room like a bathroom or laundry room, so when she poops on one area she can walk to the other side of the room until you can go in and clean it. This is easier than cleaning the entire crate and the dog.

As you do dog sitting over the years, you will be able to identify dogs who don't look healthy.

I have a small medicine chest that contains Children's Benadryl, Pepto Bismol tablets and antacids. I have a jar of peanut butter that makes it easy to administer pill medication, and I have cans of pumpkin, and chicken and rice, for upset stomachs.

6(ﾟ∀ﾟ)o

Furniture

You are not able to own nice furniture in your dog area. Get that thought out of your mind. You will be training puppies, and puppies will chew and scratch and poop on everything eventually.

Let's start with my "space" couch. My wife calls it a space couch, because it is a normal couch, but because of the wear-and-tear, I nailed a vinyl tarp over the face of the couch, to cover up stains and make it look clean. I also love the tarp because it doesn't allow things to fall into the cracks of the couch. The vinyl tarp is easy to clean and when it gets too dirty or rips I just spend another $20 and get another tarp and nail it on over the others. This happens about every six months or so. It sure beats buying a new thousand dollar couch every year.

I allow dogs to sit on the couch and so the couch gets a lot of wear and tear.

Perhaps my favorite furniture pieces in the living room, are two tables that have caster wheels on them. These wheels allow me to move the tables around, to block dogs from intruding on my personal space.

So for example let's say I invite my wife into the living room to watch a movie. The dogs will naturally want to pester her because she's new and interesting. So while we are watching the movie, she will move the rolling tables in such a way as to block the dogs from her. If the dogs are still annoying her, I will put them behind the baby gate.

My personal electronics are well protected from dogs and puppies. All the wires of my big screen TV, cable box, Wi-Fi router, modem, and the power strips to the stereo sound system, all those wires have been carefully routed along the baseboards, and pinched off by big furniture, or 5 gallon buckets, or pillows that I stuff in small areas. Curious puppies.

I keep things like scissors, pens, dog nail clippers, business cards, etc. in clear Tupperware storage boxes with locking lids. These are stackable boxes and the dogs should not mess with these boxes.

For waste baskets in the dog area, I use a 5 gallon bucket with a locking plastic lid. Don't put food in these buckets or curious dogs might try to get inside.

I keep the dog treats on a high shelf approximately 4 feet from the ground. You might be thinking that some dogs can easily get to the treats and I should keep them higher off the ground. I feel like the dogs need to respect my home, and so these are plainly "my treats," and my area, and if I catch a dog up there he's going to get corrected and given a big time out.

The same goes for my baby gate that separates my upstairs from my living room. This baby gate can easily he pushed aside by any dog. Even a small dog can push it and get behind it. But the gate is a symbol of my control, and they must respect it. If I catch them upstairs where they're not supposed to be, they will get corrected and a timeout for breaching the baby gate.

It is important to keep your house clean. If your furniture is starting to look run down because of the wear and tear of so many dogs, you might want to take it outside and give it a good spray paint. Yes, it will look like a cheap spray paint job, but that is preferable to looking at dirty tables and chairs.

Dog beds are important to have. The best way to get a dog bed is make sure it doesn't have fleas or eggs or bed bugs. Then you want to wrap it in a big contractor trash bag to protect it from pee and poop accidents. Then you will cover the dog bed with a fitted sheet. I love the fitted sheets because it's harder for a dog to remove it.

You will probably want to paint your walls every couple years as the dog slobber and mud tends to stain the walls before long.

Having carpet or rugs in a dog area is a bad idea. The exception to that are small rugs that I use almost like pee pads.

If I put a small rug by the doggy door, and a puppy is unwilling to go out the doggie door because of bad weather, she will probably pee or poo on that rug, and that is actually easier to clean than if she pooped on the floor.

I have 2 exercise pens in the dog area, and I have three crates ranging from a three-foot-long crate, to a 2 ft long crate, to a 1 foot long crate. I use the exercise pens frequently. They are roughly 4 ft by 2 ft and they have no wiring on the top.

This is where the dogs will go for time outs, when they misbehave or need a correction. There is a dog bed in each exercise pen, but if the dog is presenting destructive behavior, like chewing up toys, I will remove the bed if I feel the dog might destroy it. I will also remove the dog bed if the dog is covered in mud or is wet from the rain.

Your doggie door is an important part of your home. I don't know that you can do this business without a doggie door and a fenced yard. During rough weather I close the doggie door, because I'd rather teach the dog to hold it during the storm, than for them to go out in a serious storm and risk their life.

When your doggie door starts to look worn out, you can buy replacement flaps, and you can also paint and replace the entire doggie door to keep it looking clean and neat.

When the dog exits the doggie door and goes into the yard, I have a ramp that slowly leads to the yard. The ramp has wooden rails,, like tiny steps, to help with the grip of the feet. I live in a snowy and icy climate, and the reason for the ramp is to make it easy for old dogs and young puppies to walk easily in and out of the doggie door, even if there is snow and ice on the ramp.

I am constantly sweeping snow off the ramp, and applying ice-melt salt. I personally prefer the salt melt over the pet friendly version, but you can use whatever suits your needs.

I have certain items in the home that I call "decoys." It's almost like they are bait traps for a dog. I have a basket that has been chewed on by many dogs, it is a straw basket. It is obviously in an area that the dogs are not allowed in. Eventually every puppy will go to the basket and sniff around, and I will tell her "No!" She has to learn to respect my "No!" If she continues to mess with the basket, she will get corrected and get a time out.

Having this many dogs is going to create a lot of dander, hair, and dust. You will need to change your furnace air filter once a month. You will also need to dust your house frequently. For this I use air compressor hose. I used to work as a handyman, and the fastest way to clean a room after major construction, was to take an air hose and just blow all the dust off of everything and onto the ground. This is the most effective way of cleaning a room, ceiling fans, and high shelves.

Again I should say that if you are in the dog business, one sacrifice you have to make is that you cannot have expensive and fragile furniture.

For example, I do not like having raw glass in the dog area. For years my wife had this bookcase that had a raw glass door on it, and we kept it in the dog area. I never stopped worrying about that glass. My fear was that a dog would bump it and break it, then the broken pieces would be on the floor and other dogs would walk over the glass and cut their feet.

You should not have anything fragile, poisonous, or flammable in the dog area.

Don't let dogs get too close to your drapes and curtains. Dogs often have separation anxiety when they get dropped off at the dog sitters house. If you allow a dog to post itself at your window, scanning the streets for its owner and barking at anything it sees, she could ruin your drapes and disturb the natural peace of the home.

I have a big glass storm door in my front door. Sometimes I like to open the door, and keep the storm door locked and closed, so the dogs can sit and watch traffic as it goes by. But if a dog cannot handle this responsibility, I will simply close the door.

In my home, I have my diploma certificates and newspaper articles all framed on an "achievement wall," that people will see when they first come into the home. This immediately sets a tone. People know that I take my job seriously, that I've had some training, they see the newspaper articles and the Awards and they feel better about doing business with me.

I have a plastic chest of drawers that is lightweight and yet difficult for dogs to destroy. In these drawers I keep heartworm medicine, extra collars and harnesses, little jackets and sweaters for the puppies, extra leashes, and things like that.

I keep my cleaning products off the floor. My cleaning products are Lysol, either lemon or orange, and Febreze. I use clear tap water for cleaning TV screens or furniture.

ᘵ(˙ ˳ ˙)ʊ

Chewing Behavior

Chewing is one of the most frustrating bad habits a dog can have. Usually this urge is strongest in puppies, and so you will be dealing with this problem often.

There is the normal type of chewing behavior, which itself is very destructive and needs to be corrected. But then there is heavy duty destructive chewing, where a dog can totally destroy a hard rubber toy, a dog bed, your favorite shoe or your cell phone.

If a dog shows chewing behavior, I will correct her firmly, give her a timeout for 15 minutes, and afterwards I will give her an appropriate chew toy. If she's a small puppy, I will give her an over-sized rawhide, while she is in the exercise pen. I cannot give her that type of a chew toy around other dogs, because they might take it from her. Then you might see food aggression or resource protection.

Sometimes a dog will have such destructive chewing behavior, that she will swallow ingested pieces of plastic, she could tear up a dish rag or piece of fabric and eat it. One dog successfully swallowed an entire dish rag, and the surgery to remove the dishrag cost $3,000.

I really hate using the electric collar. In fact I only use it for two reasons. Aggressive dogs and destructive dogs. And in both of those situations I only use it when nothing else works. I will exhaust all other options before I use an electric collar. In fact, I store my electric collars in my basement, because by putting it far away, I am forcing myself to walk over there and think about what I'm doing. Is this really necessary? Have I truly tried every other less painful method?

Sadly, if you have a dog who is destroying things in the home, the only thing I know that truly works is the electric collar. It probably won't work on 1 zap. You will probably have to give four or more separate zaps before the dog understands and stops.

Dogs will try to test you. You have to be consistent in your response in order for the dog to understand. Your behavior should always be one of compassion, love, and patience with the dog, where you are giving her treats, affection, and praise.

But when she breaks a rule, you automatically become disciplinarian, you correct the dog, you put her in the exercise pen, and you don't come back until it's time to let her out.

Sadly, when it comes to chewing, usually the collar will have to come out.

You have to remember that you are saving the dog's life by using the electric collar. Do you honestly think that if you don't solve this chewing problem, she can live a happy normal life with her owner? No. Not possible. What will happen is, this dog will eventually chew something and piss her owner off so bad, that the dog will be given to a shelter. This could lead to even worse behavior from the dog, and the dog could even be executed. 3 million dogs are put to death each year in the U.S., and destructive chewing is a major reason.

I want to remind you of your place in the dog's world. You are practicing tough love. You love these dogs, and that's why you are willing to correct their behavior. You understand that the dog cannot exist without a person who loves it. And if that person is seeing aggressive behavior or destructive behavior like chewing, the owner will not love the dog as much, and the dog is highly likely to end up in a shelter.

So when you see destructive chewing behavior, how should you handle it?

First go charge the electric collar. I will put the collar on the dog, and then I will bring the dog to the spot where she destroyed something by chewing. When she's there I will hold her and show her what she did, and I will scold her so she feels bad. Next I will let her go and I will give her a zap full strength. She will probably yelp and run outside.

I don't want her to feel like I'm attacking her. I am not attacking her, I am correcting her, so I will give her five or ten minutes outside on her own, and then I will go outside and invite her back into the house, as if she is part of the pack. I still love the dog, but I do not love the chewing behavior, and that is what I'm trying to impress upon her.

You can decide to leave the electric collar on the dog during the day, and if so you can probably catch her chewing on something she should not, and give her a zap. This is super effective.

The way I like to do it is, I keep the collar downstairs. I only get it as a last resort, and I make sure I'm not overly angry at the dog. I put the collar on, put her in the exercise pen, and then I bring the pieces of whatever thing she destroyed by chewing. I show it to her, and I say "No!" I say this over and over. I give her a zap and maybe more, depending on how many times she has destroyed something in my home. I want to escalate the discomfort based on how many times she has broken this rule.

Trust the dog to be intelligent. Pain is a powerful motivation, perhaps the most powerful motivation in the world.

Another technique you can use is the put a muzzle on the dog when you can't be with her.

If a dog comes to your house for puppy training, she better not be chewing on things when she graduates. If you need to ask for an additional week of training, that's better for you, than if you let the dog go home and she chews up something valuable. This behavior is not impossible to correct. Do what I'm saying here in this section and you should see the dog responding by the third or fourth zap from the collar.

Don't go crazy zapping the dog. Don't lose your cool. If the dog looks like she is in trauma, stop.

ᕕ(͡° ͜ʖ ͡°)ᕗ

Pit Bulls

Let's talk about pit bulls, in my opinion the most dangerous dog on Earth.

I do not allow pit bulls in my home. I am always cautious of pit bulls when I see them on the street. I have seen pit bulls kill other animals, many times, so my experience with pit bulls is not imaginary. I saw the destructive power of this breed, and for that reason I stay away from them.

There is no safe way to do a dog business and accept pit bulls. Pit bulls are way too dangerous to have in your home. The Pit bull was bred specifically to kill. This dog has an unusually high tolerance for pain, and this dog has absolutely no fear.

You're running a dog business. Puppies, old dogs, slow, fat, gentle dogs, that will panic, and hide under the sofa if you brought a pit bull into your home.

And you may actually be reading this book with the idea of dog sitting for pit bulls exclusively. This is a really really bad idea. Because the only thing worse than one pit bull in your home, is two or more pit bulls in your home. Now you have a straight up dog fight, and all you need is some drunk idiots gambling and you have Michael Vick Thunderdome.

Be careful when you go to dog parks. Pit bulls are allowed there legally, and there is every likelihood that you will meet one there. I personally recommend that you do not bring any dogs that is in your care to a dog park. It is better to find an empty meadow, or an old unused tennis court, or maybe a fenced-in construction site. Dog parks are dangerous because of the pit bull.

When I walk my dogs on the leash, I always have a canister of pepper spray in my front left pocket. I periodically check the pepper spray to make sure it's working properly. I do not want to have to kill a pit bull, but if the dog attacks my dogs, I promise I will give it lethal force. I don't care if the owner cries or threatens me with a gun. I will defend my dogs even if that means killing a pit bull.

And that's why I carry the pepper spray. Because I don't want to have to kill a pit bull. I want to simply incapacitate him, and make him harmless, instantly, and that's what the pepper spray will do. There is a good chance that the dog will be slow to respond to the pepper spray's effect. In other words, I may still have to kick and beat this dog, even after pepper spraying it.

I am being honest with you because I want you to be smart out there. I know some of you will recoil with what I'm saying. I also know that some of you reading this book live in places like Detroit, Flint, or Chicago, and pit bulls are everywhere. They are super dangerous, and if I don't tell you about the risks, you will get one of your dogs killed, or you may get bit yourself.

Pit bulls are often seen as stray dogs wandering the streets. This is because they are such strong survivors that once they escape a yard, they will roam as a stray and still survive. These dogs are the most dangerous to you, when you are walking your leash dogs. As soon as you see the pit bull, whether he is on a leash with its owner or stray, your pepper spray should be in your hand with the safety off.

I always lock eyes on the dog and never on the owner. I will let the owner know by my face in my body language that if that dog comes near me, I will kill it, definitely, and then I will turn my aggression on the owner. I am the big pit bull in this fight. I am protecting the dogs I love, and that means I'm willing to bring lethal force.

You might think that I am overreacting. I invite you to go on YouTube, and search for videos of pit bull attacks. There will be about 6 million videos, but you only have to watch the first thousand or two ,before you start to understand that these dogs are super dangerous, and they will eat you if they get a chance.

Some of you are probably thinking about pit bulls that you know, that are sweet lovable bundles of affection. Yes, definitely, I agree. There are some pit bulls that are sweet and gentle and friendly. The trouble is I cannot tell a friendly one from a deadly one. Neither can you, until it's too late.

So let's say that you think it's okay to accept a pit bull in your home, because you know the pit bull, and you know the owner, and the dog is actually friendly. Okay. Here's what's going to happen. When an owner brings her little Yorkie, or her Maltese, to your home, and she sees a pit bull in your home, she's going to turn around and leave in fright. You will lose three customers for every one pit bull you accept.

Plus you will have another problem. Once someone sees a pit bull in your home, they will attempt to bring their own pit bulls into your home. You will have to decline those pit bulls, and then the clients will say that you are unfair, because you accept some pit bulls and not others. And if you accept more than one pit bull, you are going to have a really nasty dog fight at some point.

When a lady calls me on the phone and asks me about dog sitting, I ask her what breed of dog she has. If she says pit bull, or American Staffordshire, or American Bulldog, I tell her that my insurance does not allow me to accept that breed.

So I will refer this lady and her pit bull to a local kennel. If the kennel is full, she can go on Rover.com and find a sitter. I have no problem referring a pit bull to another sitter on Rover. It's not like I'm doing them any favors, giving them my rejection dogs.

Sometimes I imagine my competition with the most difficult dogs that I reject, and I feel bad. But at the end of the day they decided to accept that dangerous breed and I did not.

When I first started dog sitting and puppy training, I lived near Detroit and Flint. There were dog fights, and people bred pit bulls primarily for protection, not affection. These dogs stayed outside, even in sub-zero temperatures. They were never loved or cared for. So many of them were chained to a tree outside, and were abused, and they went insane from all the neglect and abuse.

I have seen men get attacked by pit bulls, I've seen them destroy a cat or another dog in just a split second. In fact I think I'll tell you two stories about pit bulls.

There was a dog, a pit bull named Ozzy. Ozzy was one of those huge pit bulls, he looked like 80 lb or more. He was so fierce looking, that when I would walk him on a leash through an apartment complex, people would run inside their house and lock the door. He was so scary, people would shout at me, from far away, "Hey! Get that dog out of here!"

Ozzy never had any structure or discipline at all. His owner worked long hours and was never home. His wife was old and struggling with an illness, and she could not do much to help with the dog. This dog was so violent, that he would attack the other dog he lived with, just for practice. Everyone lived in fear of this dog, and so I was called as the dog trainer to see if I could help.

Ozzy ended up getting a prescription for daily Xanax by the veterinarian. This dog was only safe when he was on this hardcore medication. If he was sober and drug-free, I would not be willing to go into his home, and I'm his trainer.

When I was a child, the next door neighbor had a Tiger-striped pit bull with the brindle pattern. The dog was named Tiger, and Tiger was small, maybe 35-40 pounds.

This Tiger was so deadly! He would dig underneath the chain link fence easily, when his owner went to work. Then he would go through my yard and out the front gate where he would start his killing spree. We would find him by following dead bodies, and the sound of people crying. Everywhere he went, he left a trail of death. And here's the weird part. Tiger was not angry. He thought he was playing with his victims. When he grabbed a cat, and shook it, within a minute or two there's really nothing left of the cat, but bloody bits of fur scattered around. A truly lethal dog.

We used to test Tiger's strength, by putting a solid 2 x 4 in front of his face and annoying him until he would bite onto the 2 x 4. Then we can lift him off the ground and his jaw was still locked to the 2 x 4. Eventually it was the 2 x 4 that surrendered and broke into splinters.

YouTube videos about pit bull attacks are so uncomfortable to watch. If you ever find yourself in The unlucky position of being attacked by a pit bull, here's what you need to remember. They are most vulnerable in the eye sockets. You're going to have to grab their ear and use your thumb to poke their eyes out of their head. It won't be enough if you just irritate their eyes. Don't be a softie. Or you will die. Poke that dog's eyes out if you want to live.

When I was a new sitter, I made the mistake of putting in my advertisements, sorry, no pit bulls. I would get hate mail from pit bull activists, claiming I'm a dog racist.

They will always tell me that these dogs are lovable and friendly and it's all about the owner. I totally agree. But bad owners exist, and they are everywhere, and I simply don't have the time or patience to filter out all those bad dogs and bad owners. So my policy is to say in advertisements, "friendly dogs only." But what that means to me is no pit bulls.

The short version of this chapter is: Do not accept pit bulls under any circumstances in your home, it is not worth the risk, and if you tell your regular dog owners that you do not accept pit bulls, they will like you even more.

There are a few other breeds that I am very cautious about taking in. These breeds are on a case-by-case basis. I have to meet the dog, and watch his behavior, and make sure I'm comfortable with him. These breeds include Doberman, German Shepherd, and Rottweiler. The Chow has a nasty reputation as well, but the breed has such little popularity now, that I only ran into one Chow in the last 5 Years.

6(˘ ౪ ˘)o

Home Ownership

I want to talk for a minute about home ownership. I do not believe this type
of business can be done as a renter.

When I purchased my home, I had to make major structural changes to the
property, in order to accommodate a dog business. I have a huge set of barn
doors in my home, to block off dogs from the kitchen area. I have a 6 foot
chain link fence that I had to install, to keep the dogs secure in the yard. I
installed the doggie door and the sloping ramp that leads up to it.

Home-ownership is essential for this business. If I had a landlord, he would
probably object to me having 10 dogs in his rental property.

I have a friend who is a breeder, and she is also a renter. She has to hide the
puppies from the nosy neighbors, who complain about the smell of urine, and
the constant whining and barking. She has been threatened with eviction
more than once. Don't let this happen to you.

I would rather live in a rundown Detroit-looking home that is MY home,
because I own it, than an extravagant rental property, where I am a tenant and
not a homeowner. The dog business is simply not a possible option if you are
not the homeowner.

The exception to this is purchasing on a land contract. If you are renting to
own, you will have much greater control over what actions are permissible on
the property. For example, you will be able to install a tall fence to keep the
dogs safe. You will be able to install a doggie door without any hassle. And
if you had 10 dogs on the property that's your personal business and not a
concern for your landlord.

Another reason home-ownership is essential, is because the homeowner is
responsible for maintenance of the property. So if a dog destroys a part of
the laminate floor, I will replace that floor section at my cost. But a tenant
would never do that, because it's not his floor, and it's not his property, and
that is a problem, because the landlord doesn't want to fix that hole in the

floor because it was done by your dogs and your business.

Home ownership is not only essential for the dog business, it's essential for peace of mind in general. I remember how I lived as a tenant. I never felt like I was permanently in any one place. I always felt pressured by the landlord, complying with his rules, and making sure he got his rent on time, and all of the hassles that come with being a renter. The peace of mind and security of being a homeowner is one of the most pleasant feelings you will ever have.

You definitely don't want to do this type of business in your mom's home, or a trailer park, or a home that is next to a busy highway. If your home is in a high crime area, you may have a difficult time attracting clients.

૮(⸝⸝ • ༝ • ⸝⸝)ა

Traveling Dog Sitters

When I watch dogs in my home, I am called an in-home dog sitter. But a person who travels in their car to a clients' home, and sits in their house, like a house sitter, that is a traveling dog sitter.

My advice is for you to never do traveling dog sitting. There are several reasons.

First of all, you can't be in two places at once. So if you are a traveling sitter, you can't be an in-home sitter, because you will be neglecting one group of dogs, every time you watch the other. This is horribly unprofessional.

The next reason you don't want to do traveling sitter work, is because of the immense impracticality of it all. When you drive 50 miles to get to a client's home, are you going to bring food, toiletries, and entertainment? Are you going to sleep in your car, or in the person's home? Do you feel safe, spending time in someone else's home, a stranger? It all sounds very uncomfortable and unpleasant.

The last reason you do not want to be a traveling sitter is because you would have to charge so much that almost no one would be able to pay it. Let's do the math. If I have 10 dogs in my home, at $25 a day, that's $250 a day. But if I agree to watch a dog at a client's home, there is only one dog at that home, so to earn the same amount, for the same days work, I would have to charge $250. And that doesn't include gas and travel time. Travel time is huge because if it takes me an hour each way to the client's home, that's an hour I have to charge for that time.

One time I had an exception to this rule. A friend of mine had two large mastiff dogs and they needed walks, 3 times a week. I would drive 20 minutes to their home, and walk them around the block. This was more of a friendship thing then a financial decision. There were many times when I wanted to stop walking those dogs, but it was my love for the dogs, and my friendship with the owner, that kept me doing it for years. I would not do it again, because it took a lot of extra effort, to schedule my day to include those walks in the middle of the day, and the commute.

 Another service I do for my clients, is I offer to meet them halfway to pick up their dogs if they live very far from me. I charge for this service, for travel time and gas. I only offer this to clients who have been loyal to me for many years. This is also a friendship type of thing I do and not standard practice.

6(ˉ‧ ˴ˉ)ʊ

Storing Dog Food And Property

When a dog first comes to your home, she will come with a leash, some dry dog food, some treats, possibly a few chew toys, and sometimes even a dog bed or crate.

Let's start with the dog food. The dog area of my home has a small half-bathroom. I use this bathroom as a mini kitchen and dry food storage. This is where I keep all the dogs' dry food. I have to keep dry food behind this closed bathroom door, because some dogs are food obsessive, and they will climb up a shelf, or leap on top of a table to get to the food.

As soon as the dog comes into the home, I put the dog in the general area, and make sure she is accepted, and friendly with the other dogs. Then I return, and I put all the personal property in a white plastic grocery bag. I use a fat magic marker to put the dog's name on it.

If the dog comes with a crate or a dog bed, I do not put those items in my general dog area, because I already have my own dog beds and crates to use. But I will store the client's property in the back room. I will write the dog's name on a white plastic grocery bag, and put that bag in the crate or tucked into the dog bed for easy identification. I will also put the dogs leashes and other personal items like medication, chew toys, medical papers, etc., in the same bag. This way I never lose any of the dogs' property.

You have to be really careful with mixing the dog foods up. If you give a dog a dry dog food that he is not used to, he will have bad diarrhea.

All the dog food in my bathroom is marked with the dog's name on it. I use heavy towels and clothespins to keep the dog food bags closed.

When I do my feeding, I want to get in and out fast, get everyone fed so that the feeding is over quickly. I accomplish this by mixing a little bit of wet dog food in each dog bowl. This flavor excites the dogs and they eat it up quick. If there is anything left after the feeding, I throw it away in a 5 gallon bucket that has a locking lid on it. This bucket is kept up off the ground, to discourage dogs from messing with it.

Never feed dogs together unless you know them very very well. You should not do this, it's too dangerous when you are new. Food aggression is common and dogs will bite each other to protect their food.

When I do my feeding, I put each dog in a separate area. I use baby gates, crates, room doors, and exercise pens, to separate every dog so they can eat without intrusion from another dog. You have to do this or you will get dogs biting each other over food.

My wet dog food is either Alpo or Purina gravy flavors. These brands are popular, affordable, and the dogs really respond to them. I use a plastic cap that fits on the top of the cans, so I can refrigerate the leftovers and use it the next meal.

Sometimes a a dog owner will give you several toys with the dog. My advice is to take the hard rubber durable toys and let them play with it.

If any dog gets possessive of a toy you have to remove the toy immediately or risk a fight.

As for plush toys and fragile toys, I don't want those in my home, because the
get ripped up really fast, and I can't give back a toy in tatters to the owner.
Also I have to pick up all the plush when the dogs rip up toys. For this
reason I only want hard rubber chew toys in my home. I like tennis balls.
They are awesome, and I love those hard durable rope toys, where they can
play tug-of-war.

When a dog is about to be picked up by her owner, I will go in the back
room, grab the property bag belonging to that dog, then I will go in the
bathroom, and grab the dog's food. Next, I leash the dog, and take her
outside to meet the owner. This is usually a very heartwarming moment, the
reunions between the owner and the dog. Especially if it's their first time
away from each other, or if it was a long stay. It's very emotional and
special.

ᔕ(ˉ ⋏ ˉ)ʊ

Dog Parks

To be honest I am not a big fan of dog parks.

I think they are potentially dangerous, because aggressive dogs like pit bulls
are legally allowed to come to a dog park. I used to go to dog parks quite a
bit when I was a young trainer, but now I do not see a need.

If I want dogs to run off-leash and have fun, there is a local empty
construction lot near my home, it's a few acres but it's fenced in, and just has
old rusted equipment in there. This is where I take dogs and let them run
around. I like this better because there are no pit bulls.

Besides the risk of a dog attack, dog parks have other problems. Don't bring
a puppy to a dog park, because there's a good chance a dog with parvo has
been there at some point. Now you are exposing a young puppy with a
vulnerable immune system to parvo, the most deadly puppy disease. This is
not responsible and it could destroy your entire business.

If I was going to open a dog park, it would be members-only, private dog
park. Every member would fill out an application, and get a keycard just like
they were joining a gym, and they would get a monthly fee. This way I can
filter out any dogs that are the least bit aggressive. And I can hold owners

accountable because I have their personal information, should a dog get attacked and killed.

I read stories in the news about evil people throwing dog treats that are poisoned onto the grass of a dog park. This is another risk I'm not willing to accept.

6(￣ ̇ ☠ ̄ ̇)ᶴ

Bathing a Dog

Part of your job involves bathing a dog, when the dog rolls in poop, or has poop stuck to her fur, or when a dog is muddy on a rainy day.

I use VO5 shampoo on the dogs, because it's very cheap, at $0.95 a bottle.

If the weather is good outside, I will leash the dog to my chain link fence, so she can't move. I will bring the garden hose to her. I have a special nozzle attachment that allows me to control the pressure instead of using my finger. First, I'm going to spray off the big stuff like the mud and the poop. You should expect the dog to shake her fur and shower you with some rain LOL.

After I rinse off the big dirt, I will put a handful of VO5 shampoo on the rear of the dog and work a leather. I'll put some shampoo on a specific area if it stinks of poop or pee.

I will let the dog shake off the excess water after I rinse her. Then I will get a terry cloth towel and dry her some more. If I suspect she's going to get muddy again, I will put her in the exercise pen for a time-out.

There is a certain type of dog we called the "mud puppy." This type of dog loves to make a mess of himself in the mud, he thinks it's the best feeling in the world to beat completely filthy. This dog will also try to take a Jacuzzi dip in your water bowls, so be careful there.

In the cold winter months, when the temperature gets below freezing, I cannot use the outside hose. I dismantle the hose and connectors, to remind myself to not use it until May 1st, when the ground has thawed completely. During these cold months, I will wash the dog in my bathtub. Again, I use the VO5. I have a special shower head attachment that has a hose.

I will put the dog in the bathtub just like if he was at the groomers and give him a good bath.

I don't offer grooming as a service to clients. I only do it when the dog is covered in mud or poop, because I have no choice. If a dog has long hair and needs a haircut or a good bath, I might offer to take the dog to the groomers during the vacation stay, but I would only offer this if I was trying to help the client and I would definitely charge probably 25 bucks to take the dog to the groomer.

I don't know if it's a good idea to offer grooming service to your clients. I feel like if you are busy washing dogs, you're going to be neglecting the other dogs you are sitting for. Don't get distracted.

ᘓ(ˉ·ᵡ·ˉ)ʊ

Groomer Visit

You should really be careful when you choose a groomer to take your client dogs. PetSmart has been in the news locally, because dogs have jumped off the table while being groomed and hung themselves. There is a huge potential for a dog fight in a dog groomer situation. The dogs are nervous and the girls who work there are not always strong alpha personalities, so an aggressive dog could easily overwhelm them.

There is a lady in my town, she is about 75 years old, and she has been a groomer for 30 years. People love her and she's a sweet person, but because she's old and her eyesight and hand coordination have gotten rusty. When she cuts a dog's hair, it's a real butch cut. I love the woman, but the grooming is awful so I don't go there.

I have a special groomer I work with, I trust her to handle the dogs well, she can handle difficult dogs that show anxiety or fearfulness. I recommend you find someone that's good in your area and build a relationship with them. Check their reviews, compare their services and you should do just fine.

If you feel a dog is not behaving well at the groomers, you should not offer that service anymore to that client. The risk of that dog biting someone is not something you get paid enough to deal with.

$\omega(\overline{\cdot} \ \underline{\bullet} \ \overline{\cdot})\upsilon$

Handling a Medical Emergency

As a dog sitter you have to be aware of all possible medical emergencies, and have a plan of action for how to deal with each one.

If a dog is bleeding, you will want to apply pressure to the wound. If the blood does not stop quickly, you will continue to apply pressure and get the dog into your car, to go to the veterinarian.

If a dog has an infection, or vomiting, or diarrhea, or almost anything else, the proper procedure would be to photograph the injury or illness, and text message the owner with a detailed description of what you are seeing with the dog. If you don't hear back from the owner in a reasonable time, you will have to make your own best decision, but you did the right thing by notifying them quickly.

Even if you tell the owner what happened to the dog, most times the owner will trust your judgment as to what to do next. You will have to develop this excellent judgment, and know whether it's best for a dog to rest and recover, or visit the veterinarian.

When you visit the veterinarian, you need to inform the owner that she must call ahead to the veterinarian and make payment arrangements. If you don't do this in advance, you could be liable for the cost of the vet visit.

You have to be aware of the capacity and capability of your local veterinarian. For example, my veterinarian can handle a sprained leg or some minor stitches. But if a dog ingests poison, my local veterinarian is not equipped to test for the broad range of possible poisons. For that, I will go 50 miles away to the local University, whose Animal Hospital is the best in the state. They will charge a little more, but they will save the dog's life, and you won't waste valuable time at the local veterinarian.

My local veterinarian would not be the best place to take a dog with an eye injury. Again, for specialized treatment like this, I would go the extra distance to the university Animal Hospital.

If a dog has diarrhea, you need to monitor her condition. If you see any blood in the stool, that the cause for alarm. If you see any mucus, that is also a problem. You would follow the same procedure, informing the owner, and asking her what she wants you to do. If she asks you to take the dog to the veterinarian, you will do so.

After a dog returns from the veterinarian, she will need time to rest and heal. You should put her bed in a separate area, so other dogs can't bother her.

When a dog is at my home, I may notice things about the dogs health that the owner has not noticed. For example, I may be petting a dog and notice a lump under the fur. This could be a possible tumor. It's not for me to diagnose anything, it's just my responsibility to tell the owner that I discovered a lump. She may have already had it examined, or she may ask about it the next time she goes to the vet. It's my job to tell the clients anything I discover about the dogs health.

To be honest I don't do a whole lot of emergency trips or phone calls. I keep my house safe and I keep my dogs healthy and that's why I don't have many emergencies.

Rover.com has a policy whereby you have to notify them of any injury to a dog, just the same as you would contact the owner. There is a Rover hotline that you can call and let them know what's happening with the Rover dog.

ᕙ(˘ ‸ ˘)ᕗ

Electric Collars

First, I want you to notice that I called these collars “Electric.” I do not call them shock collars or training collars. “Shock collar” sounds cruel, and “training collars” does not sound cruel enough to describe this type of device.

Next, I want to point out that these collars are everywhere now. Millions of people have an Invisible Fence in their yard, and this is a type of electric collar. There is an electric wire perimeter around the house, and if the dog, who is wearing an electric collar, strays too close to the wire perimeter he will get a zap.

These collars also exist in the form of bark collars. A bark collar is worn by the dog and it detects vibrations in the throat area. If the vibration is a certain intensity it will give the dog a zap.

The last collar is the one I use the most, it is the standard electric training collar.

I only use the electric collar in 2 situations. I use it for aggressive dogs, and I use it for dogs who are destructive, which means they are chewing stuff up or destroying property in the home.

I feel like destructive behavior warrants a serious response. Honestly I have not seen anything else that works for certain destructive dogs.

I will only use the electric collar when I have exhausted all other possible training techniques. I will use the time out first, then I will use a dish rag to spank the dog. If the dog still does it stop with the aggression or the destructive behavior, I have no choice but to put the electric collar on her.

Here are some tips for using the electric collar. First, don't put the collar where you can easily reach it. You should put it far away from the dog area. It is a tool of last resort.

When I need the collar, I have to walk down into my basement to get it. This gives me a few seconds to think about what I'm about to do. I can damage the trust between me and the dog with this device. I also put all the other dogs in the home in a sense of dread and panic, because they will hear the dog yelp when she gets zapped, and that causes them stress.

At the same time, the other dogs are watching me. If they see an aggressive dog challenge me, and not back down, they may challenge me as well. But if they see the dog act aggressively, and then get zapped and back down, they will understand that aggression is a bad idea.

I feel awful when I use the electric collar. I just don't like to hurt dogs. But I've been doing this business for a long time, and I know that aggressive dogs almost always end up in the dog pound, where they are executed. So I am introducing a little discomfort in their lives today, to prevent an execution in the future.

The same applies to the destructive dog. There is no one I know who is willing to home a destructive dog. No one wants to come home and find their personal clothes and furniture all shredded up by a destructive dog. These dogs also end up in the dog pound, and almost certainly get put down rather than adopted.

If you are inclined, you can sell the invisible fence as something that you can install for the clients. When I was a new dog trainer, and an owner said they had no fence at all, I would offer to install an invisible fence for them, and charge between $200 and $300. You have to rent a cable burying trench digging device, at the Home Depot or Lowe's. You cannot use this machine in freezing temperatures because it won't break the frozen ground. With a trench cable digger, you can do a standard size yard in about 4 hours.

I like the electric bark collars. I never have to use them in my home, but I have them if I ever need them. You simply turn it on, set it to the desired setting, and when the dog barks, one of three things could happen. They can get a zap, or they can get a beep warning, or they could get a vibration like your cell phone vibration. Any of these things can be effective in distracting the dog from barking. Usually, the way they work is, first they will give a beep warning, then a vibration warning, and finally a zap. I like this setting the best.

With the electric collar, it has to be on the neck tightly to make good contact. For that reason it appears to be uncomfortable for the dog for long periods. I don't like to leave the color on the dog's neck too long.

I will see the aggressive dog, put him in the exercise pen, and turn on the collar and put it on him. Then I will give him a zap. I will set the collar to the least powerful setting that will give me the dogs full attention. It is acceptable if the dog yelps.

If you use the collar, I recommend taking it off after the dog has totally calmed down. Be careful reaching in there too soon, or the dog may bite you.

If you use the collar too much, you could lose the trust of the dog. Then you will have to slowly build that trust back up. It is best not to go too heavy with the electric collar, so as to not destroy the trust between you and the dog. After I zap a dog, I will wait for things to calm down between us. When I am sure he is relaxed, I will remind him why he got zapped by saying "no fighting!" Then I will slowly and carefully reach in the exercise pen and remove the electric collar. Now the dog is free to go and play again.

If the dog immediately goes out and becomes aggressive again, I will do the same exact steps, except this time I will increase the intensity of the zap. I may turn up the intensity of the zap or if he is already at maximum intensity I will give him 2 zaps, possibly more.

I am looking for signs of physical stress on the dog. Excessive drooling, panting or whining is a sign that you should stop zapping completely. If the dog pees or poops himself, that is also a clear sign that you need to stop immediately.

I want to remind you now, that we are in this business because we love dogs. Just like children, dogs need structure, and a firm hand when they are doing dangerous behavior. That's why this collar is only used for aggression or destruction. There is no other reason to use it. It is too powerful and painful to be used for anything else.

I wish I never had to use this tool. I want you to specially be careful when you're zapping an older dog, a sick dog, or a young young dog like young puppy.

6(¨ ̇ ♪ ¨ ̇)ʊ

Baby Gates

Baby gates are an important part of security and safety in the home.

I use a baby gate to keep dogs from going up the stairs to the second floor. This gate is loosely propped up against the staircase because I don't get a whole lot of dogs challenging me to go up there.

It is convenient for me and my wife to have this loosely propped up, so we can move it quickly when we need to. There is a second type of baby gate that has a latch and is actually a swinging door style, on hinges. We have one of these installed that separates one dog room from the main living room.

I keep the swinging gate open with a bungee cord hook, and I close the gate whenever I don't want dogs to follow me into another room. A great example for this is when I'm doing the feeding. Twice a day I will put each dog in his separate area, to prevent food aggression. I will use baby gates, and sometimes crates, to separate the dogs.

Sometimes I want to divide a room into two areas, to separate dogs for some reason. Maybe I am painting the walls in one room, and I want to cut the dogs off from accessing the painted area. I have baby gates that are iron fence pieces, with soft felt on the bottom, so they don't scratch my floors. If I move these gates out, they can cut a room in half.

Sometimes a dog will come to my home, and I don't feel right putting him in the exercise pen for the night. With baby gates I can separate dogs in different sleeping quarters as well.

I highly recommend that you get comfortable with using baby gates to limit the dogs' movement when necessary, and to provide safe boundaries. There are many different styles of baby gates, and you will probably sample all of them, to find the best ones for your home.

Ϥ(⁻ ᴗ ⁻)ᴜ

Doorbell

I do not like when anyone uses my doorbell, because the sound of the doorbell excites the dogs and makes them bark.

Dogs with separation anxiety are already counting the seconds before their owner returns, and the sound of the doorbell sets them into a frenzy. Then when they realize it was not their owner at the door, they get very depressed and anxious. I want to avoid all of this unnecessary excitement.

When a new client is about to bring their dog to my home for the first time, I will text them, and ask that they come to the side door of my home, and text me when they arrive, because the doorbell disturbs the dogs. In this way I'm showing my clients the best way to come to my house each day. They just text me, "I'm here," and I go outside I greet them and I bring their dog inside.

My doorbell is one of those fancy ones that has a video camera and motion sensor. I am able to speak through my doorbell and it is pretty awesome. I doubt if you will see the benefit because there is a monthly fee for this type of doorbell but if you live in a high-crime area, I highly recommend the Ring brand video doorbell system. It even comes with a service that tells you of local criminal activity in your neighborhood.

If you are training a dog, who is barking every time the doorbell rings, you can download a "doorbell" app on your phone. Then you push the button on your app, while you are standing next to the dog, and if he barks you correct him. If you do this often enough, you will desensitize him and he will stop barking.

A side issue with doorbells, is when a delivery person like post office or UPS arrives at your home.

There is something sinister about these parcel carriers to a dog. They come and go quickly, they touch the door and leave, and they never identify themselves. This drives a dog crazy!

So the dog is warning you of a potential danger. You should understand that the dog was allowed to behave this way at home, because the owners felt a need to be warned. Or, they just didn't correct it when they should have, and it became a habit. In any event, you can't allow dogs to bark in your home. It disrupts the peace and makes all the dogs uneasy.

Any dog who barks when the doorbell rings, will be corrected. They will go into the crate or exercise pen before you even open the door.

You cannot let them get away with barking just because you are distracted by the person at the door. I don't really have a problem with barking at my home, because I stay on top of it, and I don't allow it, not even a little bit.

I recommend you do the same, because barking dogs are real nuisance to your neighbors, it makes for a very unfriendly impression when a new dog is coming to your home, to be greeted with barking, makes them feel afraid. If I was bringing my dog to a dog sitter, and all the dogs were barking, I would think twice about using that sitter, because the dogs don't seem to be happy or controlled.

When your dogs are barking in the presence of a client or owner, the most correction you are able to do is to say "no barking!" You cannot correct a dog physically in front of his owner. This is why I do a structured meet-and-greet, where the dog does not meet the other dogs until the owner has left. Then I can correct the dog without worrying about the owner's reaction.

ᘳ(¯·ᴥ·¯)ᘰ

Separation Anxiety

Separation anxiety is one of the most difficult things you will deal with as a dog sitter. For some dogs, this will be the very first time they have ever been away from their owner. It is an especially stressful time for them, and you need to I know exactly how to handle these dogs.

When an animal is wild, they are self-reliant, needing only their own instincts and Nature's abundance to survive. But a modern dog is completely helpless without a human.

A dog cannot survive without a human to care for her. This makes the dog feel nervous and anxious when the human is gone, because they know they have no way of feeding themselves, or protecting themselves from danger.

My advice for a dog with separation anxiety, is to give them some space. I will use the tough love approach here. I don't want to coddle the dog, and pretend that it's okay for her to freak out. But I will not be too harsh or strict with her either.

If a dog comes into my home, and I notice the signs of separation anxiety, which are drooling of the mouth, fearful behavior regarding the other dogs, nervously sniffing the door, behaving as if in a panic state, whining, barking, or pacing, I will put that dog in the back room of the dog area. She will sit there alone, until she calms down. I may have to go in that room with her, and pet her, and give her some affection, so she feels comfortable.

Then I will slowly introduce her to the other dogs, one at a time. Let them sniff each other, and then give her some more space. If I feel this dog might be so fearful that she nips another dog, I will give her a separate yard time.

When a dog is fearful, I want to walk them with at least one other dog who is not fearful. I believe the relaxed behavior of the other dog has a calming influence on the stressful dog.

Some owners provide CBD oil in their overnight property, to be used when the dog stress is out. Sometimes it works and sometimes it doesn't. Go ahead and use it, because it cannot hurt.

If you see a dog who is expressing separation anxiety, and she is sitting in the yard, as if waiting for the owner to return, you need to disrupt that obsessive thinking. Bring her inside for a bit, have her sit next to you while you pet her, but don't let her sit in the yard, staring at the driveway. Otherwise she becomes more and more anxious, and she may start digging or trying to jump the fence.

If a dog is digging in the middle of your yard, that's a nuisance but it's really no big deal. If a dog is digging on the perimeter of the fence, that is a really big deal, because that dog is trying to escape. I recommend that you put any dog like that on a separate yard schedule, so you can monitor him, and make sure he doesn't escape.

Sometimes a puppy comes to the home, and she is experiencing separation anxiety. She is whining in the crate when you leave the room, and she's making it difficult to sleep. I find that if you put another dog near the crated dog, in another crate, the proximity will help them both relax and sleep. If the dog continues to whine in the crate, I will take a dish rag and whack the top of the dog crate menacingly, while saying, "No!" This looks fierce but the truth is, I cannot hurt the puppy, but she doesn't know that, so she gives up and stops whining.

When a puppy comes for training, the owner will often ask if she can come in the middle of the training for a visit. I discourage this, because it only makes the separation anxiety worse. Every time the owner comes to visit like this, the dog will take longer and longer to readjust to the training regimen. You should discourage these visits, as they are only helpful to the emotions of the owner, and not at all to the emotions of the dog.

The owner is going to get lots of emotional connection during the training, when you send her videos and pictures of the dog performing her basic commands, walking on the leash, and playing with the other friendly dogs in your home. This is your opportunity to help the owner relax, and not feel anxious about the separation.

Dogs become what we allow them to become. Usually, separation anxiety is complicated by the fact that the owners are usually enabling this behavior.

When I leave the room to go to the grocery store, I make sure the dogs are safe and have water, and then I just walk out the door. Maybe I will put some relaxing music on the radio, but that's about it.

For the owner of a dog with separation anxiety, their routine is usually a big dramatic scene when they leave, hugging the dog, longingly looking at the dog, telling the dog everything is going to be okay. All this fuss makes the dog nervous. Now the dog is expecting something unpleasant to happen. You should never do this.

When a dog displays symptoms of separation anxiety, you have to treat it like any other unwanted behavior. You scold her, you put her in the exercise pen, for a time out of 5 to 15 minutes.

Obviously this correction technique is not effective for a full-blown level 10 anxiety. In these cases, I have seen the dogs chewing on their own feet, chewing on the wires of the crate, and even digging into the drywall of a room, in order to escape.

When a puppy is exhibiting signs of self-harm, chewing on its own foot, nervously biting its tail, you have to make sure she doesn't injure herself. You may have to put a leash on her, and you may even have to sleep with her to monitor her. A dog with anxiety this bad should be on medication, at least have a Xanax ready from the veterinarian as a last resort.

There are two times of the year when anxiety is the worst. The first is major holidays like July 4th and New Year's Eve. Both of these holidays involve fireworks, firecrackers, drunk people, and even gunshots. This is all super stressful for certain dogs.

Thunder anxiety is just as bad. It can come anytime, just like any bad weather. Those thunder coats you see in the pet store, I am not sold on their effectiveness. You should try them anyway, just so you can know for yourself, as an expert, whether they work or not. You should never take my word for something that you can test yourself. You will be given the thunder coats by owners. Use them and judge for yourself how effective they are.

If you own a dog who has thunder anxiety or separation anxiety, I recommend Wyze remote cameras .

I use these cameras in my home. Using the app on my smartphone, I can see into each of three rooms in my home, whenever I am away from home.

What is really cool about this camera system is, I can also speak through my phone and be heard by the dogs . So I could be a hundred miles away, and I could see the dog looking agitated in the camera, and I could say, "it's okay girl, calm down..."

 There are some times when the only way I can get any rest at night, is if I sleep on the couch, holding the leash of the dog with thunder anxiety.

I also recommend playing loud music or television during thunderstorms. This will reduce the sound of the storm. When you hear the thunder strike, you should act like it's no big deal. If you act like it's ridiculous to get nervous over a thunderstorm, the dogs will soon figure out that it truly is ridiculous and they will stop feeling nervous.

ᘛ(⁻̈ ⚔ ⁻̈)ᘚ

Older Dogs

Puppies get all the attention because they are so cute. But all puppies, if they live long enough, become older dogs. Older dog sometimes require special care and we will discuss these issues here.

Sometimes an older dog will be obese. One dog that I watch, she is so heavy that she wheezes a lot. I have to take her on a shorter walk, or she will overheat. If a dog is panting frantically, you have over-exercised her.

Older dogs often have hip and joint pain. If a dog is limping, I will mention it to the owner, who probably already knows, because this is an older dog. Then I will skip her walks for a day or so, until it is safe and comfortable for her to resume daily walks.

I feel like exercise is important at every stage of a dog's life, and that includes her senior years. So I walk older dogs, even in the snow.

Older dogs are going to have vision problems and hearing problems. If a dog is old and blind, you have to be careful that it doesn't get fearful, and strike at other dogs that get near her. A dog that is this fearful will be kept in a separate area, and given outdoor time by herself.

There is one dog that I watch, she has lost all mobility in her hind legs. She wears a special harness on her rear section that helps me lift her up by a handle, and carry her outside, with only her front paws on the ground. I do what I can to help these older dogs, I love them. I myself am an older dog, and I believe in karma, so I give these dogs the love that I hope I will receive some day, when I am old and helpless.

Older dogs don't like puppies, or wild crazy behavior. If a puppy annoys an older dog, she is likely to get nipped. If you see that the older dog is distressed and disturbed, separate them.

Usually what happens is, the puppy will invite the older dog to engage in some horseplay and frolicking. The older dog will usually look away in disgust. Then they will tend to leave each other alone.

Older dogs might not smell fresh. They may be having health problems that cause them not to smell good. You can either wash the dog yourself, or ask the owner to pay for a trip to the groomer. If the dog smells bad enough, you will have to wash her somehow.

Older dogs frequently have lost control of their bladder and bowels. If a dog is not able to control her pee or poo, she should be put in the back room in a secluded area, so she doesn't poop all over the house. She should never be in a area with rugs or carpet. She should be given frequent outdoor breaks.

Sometimes you are in the unique position to give professional advice to an owner. It is not easy to decide when to put an old dog down. I personally feel that if the dog is in pain, and her quality of life is not there, it is near the time. But this is a personal decision that each owner must face on their own. Your advice can make a difference. If you see a dog in pain, suffering, uncomfortable, dementia, these are signs that the dog might be ready to be put to sleep. Life shouldn't be about agony, and there is no cure for old age and death.

One time when I was a young adult, my mother asked me to take her cat to the vet to be put to sleep. I looked at the cat, and I had love this cat, for many years, and I didn't want her to be put to sleep.

So I told my mom to wait a few days and see if the cat improves.

I said that on a Friday. That weekend the cat moaned and screamed in agony, she was in pain the whole weekend, and she drove me nuts with her screams and moans of pain. Monday morning I took her to put her to sleep. I did not do that cat any favors by increasing her agony for 3 days.

Use your best judgment when dealing with older dogs. If you don't have a heart of compassion, love and kindness, you should not be in the dog business, and you probably won't last.

ᘔ(˙ ̞ ˙)ʊ

Different Dog Breeds

Let's spend a moment and talk about the different dog breeds, and how they impact your dog sitting and puppy training business.

The Labrador retriever is a personal favorite of mine. But the puppies can be quite a handful when they are wild and untrained. Everybody loves the Labrador

My feeling on the pit bull is, I <u>never</u> accept any pit bulls in my home.

It's too risky, and the truth is I have enough business from gentle dogs, like poodles and beagles, so I don't need to accept any pit bulls. If you have never seen a pit bull attack, just Google that term, and you will see over a million horrific YouTube videos of pit bulls attacking. I have nothing against the dog but for this type of business, it is simply too dangerous of a risk.

If you accept pit bulls in your business, you better be ready for the inevitable violence that's going to result. A pit is a loaded gun, you never know when it's going to go off.

The German Shepherd is a borderline dog for me. That means that I will take this dog on a case-by-case basis. I will do a meet-and-greet, and decide if I want this dog in my home. German Shepherds are guard dogs, police dogs, and you can see that soldier mentality in their personality. They are very territorial, and if they are not trained well they can be violent. German Shepherds are superior athletes and can easily jump high fences and dig under fences.

I love the German Shepherd breed for its strength and intelligence. But certain German Shepherds who can't play nice, or GS dogs that are escape prone are not a good fit for my home, or yours.

The German Shepherd is a very dominant breed. This dog is going to be prone to rough play and aggressive behavior. You will have to be very careful. Usually with a borderline dog like this, I will do the meet-and-greet, and bring the dog outside the fenced yard, so he can see the other dogs through the chain-link fence. If he acts aggressive in any way, I will politely decline to watch him. If he wags his tail and looks friendly, I will take him inside and see how he does around the other dogs. If I see even the slightest bit of aggression, I will decline to watch him.

The same applies to the Doberman. In every way this is a very dominant breed, with high aggressive potential. You might want to refer this dog to another sitter or to a kennel.

The Rottweiler is very large dog with very powerful body. Personally I don't see the level of aggression in a Rottweiler that I see in a pit bull. For that reason I have placed this dog on the borderline list. That doesn't mean I won't accept a Rottweiler, it just means that I will interview him very carefully to make sure he can play nice with the other dogs.

When I am interviewing a borderline dog, I am asking myself a simple question. Can I control this dog? If I'm not sure, then I will find a reason or excuse to not watch this dog.

I am not a sexist person and I totally believe in equality among the genders. That being said, a woman is smaller than a man, less assertive, more likely to be soft and passive with a dog. That is perfect for 99% of the dogs. But if you are a woman who is very feminine, petite, and don't like physical conflict, then I recommend you decline to watch any of the three breeds that I considered borderline dogs.

They will be too much for you. This is not a personal slam on women, it is a simple fact that dogs like pit bulls, Rottweilers, Dobermans, and German Shepherds require a heroic amount of effort and physical strength to control the dogs. If any of these dog breeds see a reluctance to enforce the rules, they will exploit that weakness in you.

Certain dogs like to bark. The Beagle, the Schnauzer, Terriers, and of course, the anxious or nervous dog. I've already mentioned how to stop barking in your home, in another section of this book. Basically, use the standard correction technique, when you hear the barking you say, "No Barking!" And if the dog doesn't stop, he will go in the timeout area for 5 to 15 minutes.

 Sometimes pit bull owners will try to sneak a dog past a dog sitter, because they are having a difficult time finding anyone willing to watch a pit bull.

Sometimes they might call the dog a "boxer mix" or an "American Bulldog." If you get suspicious about a dog's actual breed, simply ask the owner to text you a picture of the dog.

<u>You</u> are the dog professional, not the owner. The average dog owner lives with less than 10 dogs in his entire life. You live with 30 dogs every month. So when you see a picture of a dog you should be able to identify the breed, and even the mix breeds within the same dog. Practice identifying breeds and within a few years there will be no breed you cannot quickly identify.

The Chow Chow is a very aggressive dog. I personally have never seen a Chow getting aggressive, but other dog professionals tell me to be alert for that breed. It is a rare breed and you will probably not see it. I see one Chow for every 3 years. Look for a black tongue, that is a sign of a Chow mix. The Chow was bred to be aggressive, so I would not recommend sitting for a Chow. The sister breed of the Chow is the Shar Pei, and this is another dominant aggressive dog. I would not accept the Shar Pei in my house and I do not recommend you do it either.

If you live in a cold climate, snowy and icy, you should never accept a small breed puppy for puppy training in the winter months. You will have one hell of a time getting that dog to go outside in the freezing snow.

They would rather poop inside, and deal with whatever punishment you give, than go out in the snow. Be smart. Simply explain the situation to the owner, and ask them to schedule the puppy training for the spring. Trust me, the owner will not be able to housebreak the dog during the winter. You should focus your training in the winter on large breed puppies who are tougher and stronger, and are willing to go outside in the cold and pee.

The general rule is, the smaller the dog, the more difficult will be the housebreaking. It seems like the smaller dogs lose some control over their bladder and colon.

The Greyhound was bred for running, so be absolutely sure he doesn't get out of your yard. These dogs are so athletic, they are unable to sit like a normal dog, because their legs are too tense and tight with muscles. If you are sitting for a retired Greyhound racer, look for a tattoo on the body of the dog. This tattoo can be used to trace the lineage of the dog online through the AKC. Fascinating breed.

The American Bully is a variant of a pit bull and I would not watch any bully dog. What you want to be careful of is owners who have macho personality. They will buy powerful dogs, and then they will, subconsciously or consciously, allow those dogs to express at least some of their aggressive side. This is not a good fit for your puppy business. It is unfair, unwise, and unethical to put an American Bully in the same room with a Bichon Frise and expect everyone to be happy.

Cane Corso is another dog that I would not want in my home.

The bull terrier is okay with me, I would accept this dog in my home. I would also accept Mastiff, Saint Bernards, and Newfoundlands. These breeds are very big but I don't see the violence and aggression in these breeds.

You will probably never see an Akita either. If you do, I would put this dog on the borderline list and use your best judgment

ᘓ(ﹾ ｴ ﹾ)ʊ

Rough Play

I do not allow rough play, horseplay, or "dogs will be dogs" behavior.

I never want to hand a dog back to her owner with an injury. Dogs can be vicious. They can kill each other if you don't take control. I don't want to give a piece of a dog's ear to her owner and make stupid excuses about why I let things get too far out of hand.

One problem you will see is that owners sometimes allow their dogs to be aggressive at home. Two dogs who are brothers at home may be allowed to fight and even hurt each other. Then when that dogs get to your home, they think it's acceptable to do this. Now you have your hands full, with an aggressive dog in your home.

When I see rough play in the yard, I can't allow it to continue. I train puppies, and puppies will copy the behavior of the older dogs. The worst thing in the world would be if the puppy learned aggressive behavior, while you are trying to teach her the opposite.

Usually rough play takes a moment to build up momentum. When I am inside my living room, I might hear a yelp outside, and I will immediately run outside to see what is happening.

I will look for the aggressive dog. And I will usually take a leash or a dishrag outside to smack the dog on the butt. This dog is going to go into the exercise pen for a timeout for 15 minutes. Aggression is the worst thing a dog can do in your home, so it gets the maximum penalty for that behavior, which is 15 minute time out, and maybe a little spanking with the dishrag.

If you spank the dog on the posterior with the dishrag, there is no chance you will hurt the dog. I would let Hulk Hogan hit me on my posterior with the dish rag for an hour, as this will have no real lasting effect on me. The effect on the dog is that he understands my body language, and that I am super serious about no horse play or aggression.

I don't allow any mouthing behavior on another dog. I don't allow any bully behavior. These are all precursors to full-blown aggression. If you allow this behavior to continue, you will see nips, cuts, bleeding, howls of pain. You will also see an anxious, frightened attitude in the smaller dogs, who will be hiding from bullies.

Sometimes I hear owners and dog trainers say that one dog is the "alpha dog."

This is stupid.

If the dogs were living in the forest, they would have a dog leader, an Alpha. But the dogs live in my house, so I am the Alpha.

You are the Alpha Dog! There is no other Alpha Dog, in your home, they are all beta.

They do what you tell them, because you are much stronger, much smarter, and you have their best interests at heart.

You have to display your care for the dogs, so they trust you in this Alpha role. You do this by giving them treats, affection, and by feeding them, so that they learn to trust you.

If small puppies are rough playing in my house, I can use a loud voice to stop them, or I can simply spray them with clean water from a water bottle. If this doesn't work, I will pick up a dish rag and lightly spank them on the butt.

If they need a timeout they will get one. Puppies get a little more patience from me, because they are young and still learning. Adult dogs have more potential to hurt another dog, so I don't give them as much patience, because they are adult dogs and they should know better.

As a last resort for rough play, and aggressive bully dogs, you should have an electric collar. Put that on the dog and the next time he goes outside and acts like a bully, you will be looking at him through the window, and you give him a zap. This is extremely effective to stop the behavior.

In fact, if you are unable to stop an aggressive dogs' behavior with the electric collar, that dog does not belong in your home. Any dog that does not respond to the unpleasantness of the electric collar, and is still aggressive, is too wild, and too dangerous to be in your home. You should refer that dog to a kennel or to Rover.com for a different sitter.

ʖ(¯· ɹ ¯·)ʋ

Water Bowls

I have 10 water bottles in the house total. I have 2 upstairs for my personal dogs, 2 in the kitchen area, 2 in the rear dog area, and 4 bowls in the main dog area.

I have so many bowls, because I want clean water to be always available to the dog.

Don't be fooled by clever inventions that promise a reservoir of fresh water for your dog. Your dog will use the bowls to wash his mouth out, from mud, grass and whatever else he's chewing on. Once he pollutes the water, no other dog will want to drink it.

All my dog bowls are sitting in a clear plastic reservoir, Basically a deep tray, to catch water if a dog tips the bowls over. This is to help prevent major spills. Dogs and puppies like to knock over water bowls, and if that happens I want the 3-inch high plastic container under the water bowls to capture the water. Without this additional safeguard, the water can really ruin your floor.

I have 2 water bowls in each location, so that if one is dirty or empty, the dogs will always have the other one.

In the summertime when it's hot, I take 2 dog bowls and I put them outside, near the hose. Sometimes I regret doing this because the dogs will knock over the water, or make a mud bath with it. The water bowl outside has to be carefully watched, because mosquitoes can lay eggs in the water, and you will see larva develop over a couple days. So what you want to do is, keep that water fresh everyday outside.

The same goes for the water inside. If you would not drink it, don't let the dogs drink it. The water should be clean. I don't use fancy spring water, I use tap water, but it has to be in a clean bowl. If you live in Flint, you better give your dogs bottled or purified water.

You should monitor your water consumption carefully. If dogs are not drinking from certain bowls, it could be because they have been contaminated with something. We use Lysol and other cleansers in the home, and if some chemical got in the water bowl, the dog will not drink it, but we would never know. Change the water frequently to be safe.

Upstairs I have no water faucet so I fill a gallon water jug every couple days and bring it upstairs.

If you have a dog who is sick or old, you may find it wise to include their water in their feeding bowl with their food. In this way you make sure the dogs get the necessary water when they eat.

Some puppy trainers like to withhold water in the evening for the puppy, to prevent accidents at night. I don't do this. I let them drink anytime. They have to learn to hold their pee and not have accidents.

You should always use stainless steel water bowls, because they do not get mold easily and they are easy to clean. This also applies to feeding bowls. All my bowls are stainless steel.

When you wash a dog bowl, do not use harsh detergents. If you have a residue of detergent on the water bowl or the feeding bowl, the dog will not eat or drink from it, because he smells the contamination chemicals in the detergent.

Unless the bowl is contaminated with something serious, you can probably hand wash the water bowl your self, running clean water on it and using a clean cloth to clean it further. A dog's nose is very sensitive to chemicals and that's why we don't want to introduce harsh chemicals to the bowls.

When a new client comes in the house, those bowls better be sparkling. If the water bowls are empty or dirty, the owner will assume that they are always that way. Your water bowls are a real reflection on the quality of cleanliness you have.

Some dogs drool a lot. Sometimes you're going to see a dog drink some water, and then proceed to drool half of it on your floor. I don't get mad when this happens, I just get the mop. But when a dog purposely knocks over the water, or a puppy plays in the water like it's a Jacuzzi, that is not allowed, and calls for a correction.

ᕕ(˙ᴥ˙)ᴅ

Dog Beds

My dog beds are mostly 2 foot by 3 foot long. I have a couple that are smaller, and a couple that are bigger, but most of them are 2 foot by 3 foot. These dog beds are flat, and I have 10 dog beds available. I have another five or ten in the basement, which I will bring up on busy holidays and weekends, when I need more beds.

I also have a leather futon that is about 18 in off the ground. This large futon allows dogs to sleep in the living room. Three dogs can easily fit on the futon at night. I allow dogs to sleep on my couch. At least two dogs will sleep on

the couch on a given night. Smaller dogs like puppies and older dogs can
sleep in exercise pens or crates. If a puppy is not housebroken he will
definitely sleep in the crate until he is housebroken.

My dog beds are all protected by heavy-duty trash bags, extra large
contractor size. I tie these over the beds, to protect the beds from pee stains,
poop, and to protect them from being chewed on by puppies or misbehaving
dogs.

All my dog beds have fitted sheets on them. I love fitted sheets because it
makes it harder for a dog to remove them and start chewing on the actual
bed. The fitted sheet is easy to remove and replace and wash.

When a new client is coming into your home, it's important for you to change
the fitted sheets on the dog beds. They should look fresh and smell fresh.
When no one is coming to my home, I really don't care if a dog got a mud
stain on the fitted sheet. I know it's not pee, and so I don't rush to clean the
sheet. But if someone is coming over to the house, I want to make a fantastic
first impression, and show them my house is very clean, and that means
cleaning all the dog beds. It's a simple process. I just take all the fitted sheets
off, throw them in the washer and replace them with clean ones.

If a dog pees on the dog bed, my routine is the same every time. If it's poo, I
use a plastic grocery bag to pick up the poop, and toss it in a 5 gallon bucket
near my trash cans, which are about 20 feet from my house. This way the
poop won't smell the yard.

Now that the poop has been dealt with, I will spray the plastic cover of the
dog bed with Lysol. Usually I will use the actual dirty fitted sheet to scrub
with the Lysol. After the bed has been cleaned, I will put a new fitted sheet
on it and we are good to go.

During this whole process, the puppy will be restricted to outside in the yard,
or in a crate. I do not allow a dog to watch me cleaning up his mess, because
I don't want him to think I'm his servant.

I want him to reflect on his accident while I am cleaning it. It usually takes
me about 5 minutes to clean an accident on a dog bed. Afterwards I will let
the dog back in the house and I will say, "no pee pee!" And then we are back
to normal.

Never get your dog beds from the curb of a neighbor. You may see the neighbor throw out a bed, or a couch cushion, that would be perfect for a dog bed. But how do you know it doesn't already have bed bugs on it?

If I knew a way to microwave the bed and kill the bugs for sure, I might be inclined to get dog beds from the curb. Even used dog beds in a thrift store would be suspect. It's definitely not worth saving five bucks on a dog bed, to risk bringing insects like fleas and bed bugs into your home.

ɕ(¯· ᴥ ¯·)ʋ

I Need A Break!

There are so many positive things to say about the dog business, but this is one of the negative ones.

This is a 24-hour job, 7 days a week. In fact, weekends and holidays will actually be busier for you.

I will look at my dogs each day, and determine if they require a high level of care, or “normal level.”

If it's a high-level group of dogs, I will do my workout in the house, so that I can hear the dogs and respond to them if necessary. As I write this, it's 5 a.m. because a puppy whined in the crate, and I had to let him out to go pee. If my group of dogs is small and do not require constant attention, I may feel safe sneaking to the gym for an hour.

The gym is only 2 minutes from my home, so I can squeeze in a good workout and get back before anything bad happens. Again, I would never do this with puppies that are not housebroken, or destructive dogs, or any group of dogs that was not very stable in behavior.

This job requires your constant vigilance. That's why people pay you. You cannot go to the store, or run errands, without finding someone to cover for you.

It would be highly irresponsible of you to neglect your dogs by doing personal activities. Don't let yourself get distracted. Your main job is to care for these dogs by being physically present and aware.

Another challenge about this job is you don't get to sleep whenever you want. Dogs will wake you up with their activity, horseplay, anxiety, and whining.

You should be a light sleeper, because if you sleep heavy, you will wake up to a pile of poop in the house, or something broken, because you didn't hear the warning signs.

Because this job requires my constant presence, I have designed workout, yoga, and meditation practices that allow me to be both present and aware of the dogs in my home, while enjoying some personal development.

I built my business from the ground up, and I spent so much effort and struggle to make my business successful.

So when I think about hiring someone just to sit in my home, and watch the dogs, 99% of the people I meet do not qualify to do that.

I hired a lady, she was retired, and sweet, and she is still a good friend. But when a dog pooped in the house, she did not clean it, and I had to clean it when I returned. If the dogs are fighting in the yard she will not interrupt them, because she doesn't feel it's her place, or she doesn't have the same level of responsibility that I place on my job.

I still do not have someone reliable that I can hire for short periods. I am searching for someone who is responsible, reliable, and would be happy earning $20 an hour, to watch 10 dogs, for 2 hours at a time, while I go running errands. Then I could safely go to the gym or a yoga class. I have searched everywhere for this special person, and I still have not found her.

I think it would be the perfect job for a teenager, but a teenager may not have the necessary level of responsibility and maturity.

The teenager would have to have a driver's license, in case something went wrong. The teenager would have to have an adult level of responsibility and reliability. Also I feel strange, inviting a teenager into my home to work, because it looks socially suspicious.

I like the idea of hiring a retired senior to watch the dogs, once or twice a week, while I run errands. But the seniors seem to have their own set of issues that make this partnership unlikely. The senior has health problems usually, and sitting for dogs can be physically exhausting at times. You clean, you manage them, you feed them, you walk them, breaking up fights, it's work. Not all seniors are up to this task. A large dog can easily knock down a small, frail, elderly woman, and break her hip.

I still keep my eyes open for responsible neighbors who could use some part-time income. I've already approached the neighbors that I would trust in my home, and they all declined politely. The neighbors that I do not trust, because they are a little mentally weird or simply unreliable, I would never risk the safety of the dogs with someone I didn't fully trust.

Never leave a relative in charge with the dogs unless you are absolutely sure they are responsible enough to handle it. I trust my wife to watch the dogs when I'm gone for a short time, but I don't expect her to do the things that I do when she is watching them. I want her to listen for rough play and fighting, and I'm sure she would pick up pee or poo if she saw it, but everything else is going to be done by me when I return. Don't put a heavy burden on your relatives to watch the dogs for you, or they will stop helping you.

6(⁻ ⋅ ⁻)ᴅ

Doggy Door

I don't think this type of business is even possible without a doggy door and a fenced yard.

When I imagine trying to do a dog business without a fenced yard and doggie door, it looks ridiculous in my mind. I can honestly say that if you don't have a doggie door you don't have a dog business.

We already talked about the importance of a secure fenced yard. The doggy door is such an important part of your business.

Without a doggy door, I would have to get up and open the door 100 times a day, to let dogs in and out. I would lose $$ in heating and cooling costs. This constant opening and closing the door would distract me from my other responsibilities.

Any house can have a doggy door. They have models that attach to an
existing sliding glass door. Others can be cut into a door or a wall.
Close the doggie door when the weather is bad. Rain or snow is not good for
dogs, and they will track in all the mud, and make your house dirty. Closing
the door until the worst of the storm passes is the best thing to do.

You should close the doggie door at night when it's time to go to bed. Some
dogs are nocturnal, and they will go outside at night if you allow it. They
will bark and make noise and it's not good for this to happen late at night. I
give all the dogs a pee break in the middle of the night, so there is no other
need for them to be in the yard at night.

The doggie door is going to get dirty, from the constant in-and-out activity of
so many dogs.

After about a year, the vinyl flaps of the doggie door will become worn and
dirty-looking. They are supposed to be clear and transparent, so that dogs
aren't running into each other, going in and out. You should purchase new
replacement flaps once a year so your doggie door looks clean and neat.

The longest my doggie door has ever lasted without needing to be completely
replaced is two years. My home has to look neat and clean, and a doggie
door starts to wear out in about 2 years. The doggie door I have right now is
going to be replaced the next time, probably in the next 6 months.

If you have basic handyman skills, you can cut and install the doggie door
yourself. There are excellent YouTube videos on how to do this, including
some videos made by the doggie door manufacturers.

If you have no handyman skills, you should simply hire a handyman to install
a doggie door.

If you have a solid door, the doggie door will be cut into the door frame.
Another option is to cut the doggie door into the wall of the house itself. In
this situation you have to be extremely careful not to cut a supporting beam,
electrical wires, Plumbing, etc.

Once you have installed the doggie door, my advice is to build a very slow
sloping ramp that leads to the yard itself. I live in icy climate, and puppies
and older dogs can't climb stairs that are icy and snowy. By installing the

ramp, I make it easy for any dog to go into the yard, even if the ramp is a little bit icy.

When you build the sloping ramp, make it very low gradual slope. You should install one-inch wood slats across the face of the ramp, like mini stairs, that the dog can grip with their paws. This helps in icy weather.

Doggie doors can also be installed on sliding glass slider windows. Just Google doggie doors for sliding glass doors and you will see many options the average is costing $150.

You definitely want to buy the largest size doggy door you can find. If you get an exceptionally fat dog, you may have to open the door yourself for that dog.

If you live in a cold climate, you will have to put a bucket of ice-melt near the dog ramp, and possibly an ice scraper tool.

I don't know how I could teach housebreaking without a doggy door. I believe in letting the dog feel independent and in control of his own potty breaks.

If the dog feels the urge to pee, and there is no doggy door, the dog has to think about finding me, and letting me know that she has to go outside. This is a whole lot more difficult than teaching the dog to simply go out the doggie door.

Whether you are a dog sitter or a dog owner, the doggie door will dramatically improve your life. The average dog has to go inside and outside 10 times a day to pee or poo or just exercise. Yes, you can shrink that number to one or two trips outside, but the dog will not be happy about this, holding his pee for 6 hours at a time. Be smart. Your yard has to be fenced and you have to have a doggie door in order to have a successful dog business.

Another advantage of the doggy door is that if I'm out running an errand, and the weather is bad, I know the dogs can easily come in and out. If a dog is trapped outside, because you have no doggy door, the dog can feel the full impact of bad weather and this is not healthy. If you trap a dog outside in bad weather, he might try to escape the yard.

As a safeguard for bad weather, I have a small plastic dog house in the middle of the yard. This is in case a puppy is trapped outside in the cold snow, she can find refuge in the dog house, until I discover her and bring her inside.

ʕ(̄· ᴥ ̄·)ʋ

Dog Treats

The first thing I want to stay about dog treats is, that they are practically free for you as a dog professional.

When I make an appointment with a new client, they will commonly ask me what they need to bring. I do not have any need for dog crates, dog beds, or toys. So I tell them all they need to bring is the dog's kibble food and treats.

I don't tell them what treats to bring, or how much to bring, that's totally up to them. But because I mention this, I have a surplus of dog treats. Some clients bless me with a truly generous amount of treats that I share with all the dogs.

Perhaps the most important principle in dog training is positive reinforcement. When the dogs in my home are behaving well, they are relaxed and quiet, and not causing disturbance, I will often pass out a small treat. This reinforces the relaxing calm behavior, and helps the dog understand the appropriate way to behave in my home.

If a dog is in the timeout area, he may see me giving out treats, but he does not get one. This reinforces good behavior, because dogs don't want to miss out on tasty treats, so they will tend to avoid things that put them in the time out area.

Let's talk for a moment about human food. You might be guilty of giving your dog human food.

I give my dogs human food, but I am very careful as to what I give them. I use hot dogs slices to train puppies, who are finicky and won't take a traditional puppy treat.

I like to give dogs pieces of pork chop, baked chicken, and even steak as a reward for good behavior.

Be careful what you give the dogs, because you might be cleaning up explosive diarrhea.

Diarrhea is the most unpleasant part of dog sitting, so be careful about giving them a variety of treats, or human food that is processed, and is not naked, safe meat, with no spices, or too much grease.

Hamburger is cheap and affordable as a meat, however it has a lot of grease, and that gives dogs loose stool, so be careful.

Some dogs have sensitive stomachs, and for them you want to save some grain-free treats. Certain dogs, like English Bulldog, and the Frenchie, get upset stomach unless they eat grain-free.

When you are doing puppy training, you want to select a treat the puppy likes, and stick with that same treat everyday. This will stabilize the new puppies' digestion. Do not switch treats frequently, or you will get diarrhea.

If you are training an exceptionally small puppy or tiny breed, you should use 2 calorie treats. I have even used cat treats for tiny dogs. If you don't have cat treats, you can cut a 4 calorie treat into a 2 calorie treat.

If the dog is not accepting the traditional treats that come in the pouch, you might have to substitute hot dog slices. Make the treats small enough to give the dog some pleasurable satisfaction, without the treat being big enough for him to have a small meal. If you find yourself waiting for the dog to finish the treat, before you make the next command, the treats are too big and you should reduce their size next training session.

When you are cleaning the yard, you should be aware of loose stool on the yard. Soon you will become a absolute expert in recognizing the poop on the yard, and identifying which dog it came from. Big dogs make big poops, little dogs make little poops. Older dogs make dry poops, and I have seen living worms, bits of plastic, and even carpet fragments in a dogs' poop.

When you see loose stool on the yard, you want to dial back the treats, use safer treats, reduce and eliminate human food, or all of the above.

Sometimes a young puppy is so finicky and disinterested in food, you will have a tough time training this puppy. You will have to substitute treats for praise and affection, to get the dog to do the basic commands.

Stay away from milk products! They will give dogs explosive diarrhea. Cheese and dairy are universally loved by dogs, but they will cause loose stool and even bad diarrhea.

When you have a dog with diarrhea, do not lock him in a crate. He will poop in there, and then walk all over it, and then you will have to scrub all the wires of the crate. It's a horrible mess and you will definitely have to wash the dog. If a dog has diarrhea, keep him in a very small room, and allow him to poop in one area, and then move to another area. This is the best way.

When you are handing out treats, you never forget how food aggression works. You never let a dog save his treat, because another dog could challenge him for it, and that will cause a fight.

If a dog does not immediately eat his treat, you take it away. You also don't allow dogs to intrusively get near each other when they are eating a treat. Use your body to block one dog from another dog, when you are passing out treats. Protect small dogs and puppies from bigger, hungrier dogs using your body and voice.

When you train a puppy, you will definitely see a puppy who is teething. Puppies have to chew on appropriate things, to dislodge baby teeth, and to strengthen new teeth.

I like to give the puppies over-sized rawhides because they are too big to choke on. Stay away from those pencil-thin rawhides when you're dealing with puppies. They are too easy to choke on.

They have new dog chews that are safe for puppies. They are not one solid piece of Rawhide but they are chopped fine, so as the dog works it they become small safe pieces. They also have the tougher chewy treats called Munchy Sticks. Ask your pet store professional about safe chewy treats for teething dogs.

ᘰ(ˉ·ᴥ·ˉ)ʋ

Using Gmail to Take Notes

I'm assuming you have a smartphone, as it is necessary in this modern age, to have a phone that can handle heavy social media, video uploads and sharing, multiple websites and so forth.

Let's say you were walking your dogs, and a potential client calls you. I usually let that call go into the voicemail. I have an app on my phone, "YouMail," that translates all my voicemail calls into text, and emails it to me. Whether the client is new, or a regular client, when I am walking dogs, I don't have a pen and paper to write down appointment times, and other important information, that the client is sharing with me.

For that reason, I let the call go to voicemail. When I finish the dog walk, or the car ride, I can return calls as needed, and write down the information.

When I need to remember something and I don't have pen and paper handy, I take out my phone and I send myself a message.

I use my text message on my phone, but I put my Gmail address, as if it were the phone number I'm texting. Your smartphone will understand that you want to send a text message to your Gmail.

This helps me a lot, because I can use "voice-to-text" to capture the information, and send it to myself as a Gmail message, that I can review later, when I'm not busy.

I use Gmail for all my personal notes to myself, including scheduling changes, marketing ideas, everything. I simply text myself a message, that ends up in my Gmail account, and it is so efficient.

ᘓ(ˉ・ x ・ˉ)υ

Daily Walks

I believe that daily walks are super important, not only for the dogs, but for my own peace of mind.

It is an important benefit that I sell to my clients. When I tell my dog sitting clients that their dog will be walked every day, at no charge, that is an added benefit that other dog sitters cannot match. This is my advantage. I always mention it to new clients, that their dog will receive free daily walks with me.

A daily walk is essential, to burn off the stress and tension of the dog. The dog is stressed out, because his owner brought him to a strange place, with strange dogs around him. If you don't burn this stress off with a long walk, the dog will resort to neurotic behavior, like barking, digging, rough play, whining, and all sorts of nervous behavior.

When I walk the dogs, I sometimes take two dogs, or even three dogs at the same time.

This is only when I am comfortable with those dogs, and I know they're going to walk in a reasonably normal pattern. When I am walking multiple dogs, I like to take a picture of the multiple group, and send it to the owners, as a way of saying, "Your dog is friendly and harmonious with the other dogs."

I use prong collars on any dog that is pulling too much for my comfort.

That includes puppies that I am training. I have a tiny little prong collar that is so cute, but it still does the job. I never use a prong collar on a puppy the first time I walk her, because she will freak out. Also the prong color is only used if a dog has already shown pulling behavior, so I would never start by using a prong collar.

My second favorite leash besides the prong collar are my leashes with huge carabiner clips on the end.

These carabiners make it super easy for me to connect the carabiner to the collar of the dog. And because the strap of the leash works as a sort of belt, if I ever get a dog who's being difficult on the walk, I can use the carabiner to loop the leash around the dog's neck, and it will act as a sort of slipknot.

But unlike a hangman's noose, the carabiner is real open and wide, the mouth of it is at least 3 inches wide, so as soon as the dog stops pulling, tension is released and there is no discomfort. I trust this carabiner leash, it is my favorite leash next to the prong collar.

When I am walking the dogs, I always take a picture of them to send to the client, so they know the dog is healthy, and I am keeping my promise of giving her free daily walks. Sometimes I will check in with the client by making a short video and talking about the dogs' present status.

When I take a picture of a dog, sometimes it's really early in the morning. I prefer early morning dog walks, because there's less traffic and distractions, and I can get it done early.

If I take a picture of a dog on the walk, and it's 6 a.m., I will schedule that message to be sent at 8 a.m. or 9 am, depending on whether it's the weekend or not. No one wants to be woken up at 6 a.m. by a picture of their dog. Be respectful that people are on vacations, and they may be sleeping late. Be mindful and don't wake them up with early morning texts for non-emergencies.

When I walk my dogs, I like to take the same route. But the truth is my route varies quite a bit, depending on several factors. First it's the dog herself. If she is a young puppy on her first walk, I will go much shorter distance. Other times my path is obstructed by the river overflowing onto the sidewalk, or the snow might be making the sidewalk unsafe. In those situations I will use an alternate path. I don't like to cross the street during heavy traffic.

I never ever use an owner's dog leash. I use my own leashes, because I trust them. You would never catch me using a retractable leash. I think they are a joke and unsafe. Some owners use these cute leashes and collars that are basically fancy pieces of string, and if you are not careful those leashes and collars could break during a walk. Be careful.

Some dogs have this trick that they want to show you...

They will walk on the leash and start to slow down, so that they are behind you. If their head is smaller than their neck, they will be able to slip the collar and get away from you.

You need to check the tightness of the collar, and if you don't trust the collar, you should either tighten it, or loop the leash around the neck, like a slip knot, using a carabiner end. If you can't do that, simply use a prong collar of the appropriate size.

I have 4 prong collars, and they are all hanging next to the rear door of my home, on pegs. I keep leashes attached to them, to make it easier in the mornings when we walk. The color of the leashes tells me the size of the prong collar.

They are arranged according to size. So when a dog comes to me, ready for the walk, I will pick the appropriate size prong collar and put it on.

When you are walking your dogs you should be very mindful of your neighbors.

Your neighbors can see everything you do. They could easily photograph or video you. Don't be correcting the dogs harshly, or you could find yourself on the local news. Yes, neighbors will call the police on you, if you are seen abusing a dog on the walk.

Some dogs are going to test your patience. They will do everything they're not supposed to do, and they seem to enjoy driving you crazy. You need to go practice yoga, and meditation, and slow down. Become more patient if you want to be a successful dog professional.

Don't let the dogs wear your patience thin. I have a usual rule of thumb, that when the dog makes me feel frustrated, that's a good time to turn around and return home. There's no reason to go farther than that, if the dog is behaving that way.

When I walk the dogs, I always carry a canister of pepper spray in my left front pocket.

There is nothing else in that pocket, because I need to be able to reach the pepper spray lightning fast, in the event of a pit bull attack.

If you have never seen a pit bull attack, please go on YouTube, and watch the first 1,000 videos of pit bull attacks. You will see how horrific, deadly, and fast they are.

You will barely have time to reach for the pepper spray, and defend your dog and yourself. You should prepare yourself mentally for the possibility of a dog attack while you are walking. You are a target, because you will be walking other dogs.

Every month, you should practice spraying your pepper spray, at at a target a few feet away from you, to make sure you have your aim correct, and to make sure your pepper spray did not get old or empty.

For me, the dog walks are a therapeutic and a meditative time, a peacefulness that I truly treasure.

Nothing makes me happier than walking the dogs, and having a pleasant time of it. They love it as much as I do. It's not only an added benefit that I sell to my clients, it is healthy and it helps the dogs relax in my home. A dog who doesn't get walked at home, maybe once in a month, comes to my home and gets walked everyday. This dog sleeps better, and behaves better, because he is having his physical needs met.

When a dog owner messages me after the vacation stay, and says that her dog is sleeping for the next two days, that tells me that the daily walks had a huge benefit to the dog.

ƪ(˘・ᴥ・˘)ʋ

Security Cameras

I'm a big fan of doorbell cameras. The first one I bought was “Ring”, which was the most popular brand at the time. It kind of sucked, because there was a $10 a month fee.

There are way better doorbell cameras now. I recommend you go to Walmart and check out the reviews online. They're super affordable now starting at $40.

The way these cameras work is, it's mounted near your door, just like a doorbell. There is a camera and an audio microphone in the doorbell.

When someone approaches the door, the motion sensor will pick up their activity, and send you a notice on your smartphone app. You can see the person at your door, and you can speak back and forth to them. It is not only cool, but I think it's important, and maybe even essential, to your job as a dog professional.

When the UPS guy rings my doorbell, it is annoying. I don't open my front door, because I don't want to risk dogs running outside near the street.

I have to walk all the way around my house to get to the front door. Instead, the doorbell camera makes this trip unnecessary. I just see the UPS guy at my doorstep and I can make a mental note to pick up the packages when it's convenient for me.

Another problem I had before the doorbell camera was, if two people were picking up their dog at the same time, I would frequently bring the wrong dog to them, because I could not see them through the doorbell.

Another benefit of the doorbell camera is if a solicitor or a religious spokesman is trying to sell me something, I can ask them what they want through my smartphone, without even getting up off the couch.

I believe that in the near future all doors will have doorbell cameras. They are an essential part of home security.

There is a second type of camera that I use frequently in my home.

The Wyze cameras are super powerful, and super easy to install. They work through Wi-Fi, and connect to your smartphone by app. Wyze cameras have indoor and outdoor models, and some have very sophisticated features. I love my 3 Wyze cameras. I have one in the living room, one in the outdoor fenced yard, and one in the main dog area.

If I take a trip to the gym, I can easily pull out my smartphone, and check the status of all the dogs in my home. The Wyze cameras also allow me to speak to the dogs. So if I see any horseplay I can yell, "No!", and the dogs will hear me, and think that I am somewhere nearby. This will help them behave better.

If you have a dog suffering from separation anxiety, these cameras are super helpful. You can speak to the dog every so often, and check on the dogs when you are not near.

ᑕ(⁻ ᴥ ⁻)ᗞ

Rainy Days

Every morning I check the weather to see if rain is in the forecast.

I want to have plenty of large, clean bath towels at both the front and back door of the home.

When a dog comes in from the rain, their instinct tells them to shake their body, so as to toss off all the wet rain water. If they do this in your kitchen, you will spend the rest of the day cleaning the cupboards and appliances, from the dirty water they shake all over.

If you allow this to happen regularly, your kitchen will look much older than it is, and your house will have a dirty look and feel to it.

As soon as the dog comes in, you dry the dog with a big bath towel. I hang the bath towel over a dog crate, so that it dries between use .

When the rain is so severe that I do not want to let any dogs outside, I will close the doggie door. When I do this, I expect the young puppies to have an accident. I am not going to punish them the same way I usually do, because the rain prevents them from going outside to pee. Usually they will be near the door, and I will show them to pee, scold them and put them in another room while I clean it.

Sometimes a storm can last for days. When that happens, I look for a break in the storm. When I see a calm part of the day, I will let the dogs out altogether, make sure they pee and poo, and bring them back in, dry them off, and close the doggie door again.

When it rains super hard, my backyard turns into a mud pit! When this happens, I go next door to the gas station, and I buy two bales of hay. I spread the hay around the front of the door, covering an area of 20 ft square. This will soak up a lot of the mud, and it will clean off a lot of the mud from the dogs' paws, before they get inside the home.

You should always have a strip of floor rugs in front of the doggy door, so when muddy feet, or feet that have poop on them, will get wiped on the rugs, before they enter the main home.

If I have to leave a dog outside during extreme weather, I use my smartphone to set a timer, for 5 or 10 minutes, so I don't forget to return and bring the dog inside. Always use a timer when you are seeing extreme weather, especially when dealing with young puppies or older dogs.

When you have a thunderstorm, you should expect at least 1 dog in 20 to have thunder anxiety.

You should sit that dog near you and stroke the dog, when there is no thunder, to relax him. When the thunder claps, you should act like it's the silliest thing in the world to overreact to thunder. Your attitude of indifference will transmit a feeling of safety to the dog.

ᘓ(ᐛ •̀ ᐛ)ʊ

Phantom Smells

As a dog professional, you are going to cultivate and develop your sense of smell. Your sense of smell is going to be somewhere between that of a dog and everyone else, which means you will definitely smell pee and poo in the smallest amounts. Your sense of smell gets sharp, because you are cleaning poo and pee everyday, and looking for it.

My sense of smell is so sensitive, that I can smell a urine puddle the size of a teaspoon from a 8-week puppy. What's more, I can smell a speck of poop the size of a dime on the bottom of my shoe.

Trust me, you will develop the same sensitive nose. And that leads me to my next point. You are going to smell "phantom smells" from time to time. Poop that you smell, but cannot see. Where is this poop coming from?!?

The phantom poop smell is caused when a dog goes outside, and is playing and goofing around, and she steps in a pile of poop. Then she walks towards the home, and most of the poop falls off of her paw. But there is still enough on her paw to stain the floor of the home with a poop smell.

Another phantom smell is when a long-haired dog poops a runny poop. The poop will get stuck to the fur of the butt area, and whenever she sits on furniture, or even sits on the floor, She is wiping a little poop on that area. That is a phantom smell.

First, you want to make sure you have found the source of the poop. Check the dog's paws, and butt area, for dangling poop fragments. Take a washcloth with some mild soap, and clean those areas if necessary.

When you take a long-haired dog to the groomer, you should mention that you want the butt area shaved extra close, to prevent dangling pieces of poop.

I may not be able to identify the exact location of phantom smells, but I know when they are gone. So, if I think it's the floor in my living area, I will sprinkle 1/2 cup of Lysol on the floor, and mop the floor, and then wait to see if the smell is gone. If not, my second guess will be to spray down the couch and the dog beds. I will tackle each area until the smell is gone.

Sometimes a small dog will poop behind a cabinet or sofa or something. This is rare, but this can also cause a phantom smell. If you are unlucky and have floor ventilation grates, be careful that a dog is not able to pee inside the air conditioning grate on the floor. This is much harder to clean.

Your home should never smell like poop or pee. Never. Find the phantom smells and take care of them. If you still can't find it, after you clean everything, simply take your Febreze and spray the main areas. The good news about pee and poo is the odor diminishes over time, and eventually becomes invisible again.

$$\zeta(\overline{\cdot} \ \pounds \ \overline{\cdot} \ )\upsilon$$

Snow

Ice and snow are dangerous elements to dogs and people. We have to know exactly how to deal with heavy ice and snow as dog professionals.

When clients come to your home, it is not a good idea to have ice build-up on your driveway or walkways. If a client falls and cracks their head on your sidewalk, they might sue you, and they definitely will be upset that you did not de-ice your driveway.

I use two types of salt in my home. In the fenced yard area, I use the pet friendly ice-melt that you see in the stores. This is supposed to be safer on the dog's paws. I use this on the EZ ramp that leads to the doggie door. This is a slow grade ramp I made, to make it easy for puppies and older dogs to come in and out, even if it's icy. I put the ice-melt on the ramp, to make sure the dogs can enter and exit the home safely, without slipping.

I use traditional rock salt for the main driveway area. I feel the rock salt dissolves ice better than the pet friendly ice-melt. So I use the stronger stuff in the front of the home, because there is a great risk of a client falling.

When you are walking your dogs in icy weather, please remember that dogs make sudden moves that you will not expect. A large dog can easily pull a small person and cause them to have a serious fall on slippery ice.

Yaktrax are kind of like the spikes that golf shoes have on them. The spikes help you find traction on icy surfaces. I probably use the yaktrax two or three times a year. Most times it's not worth the inconvenience of putting on the yaktrax, because you cannot walk on a normal floor surface, as it was scratch it up.

During snowy weather, I close the doggie door, when there is a high wind because the wind will blow inside my home and make it too cold. I don't want to lose air conditioned heat from the furnace going outside through the doggie door.

Many of the windows in my home have a permanent plastic sheet that I put over the windows, on the inside. This clear plastic sheeting allows natural sunlight to come in, but it keeps the cold out. Another benefit is that people can't look directly into my home, because of the plastic sheeting, but I can see the form of a person outside, so that helps me.

I have an ice scraper tool that looks like garden hoe. I use this when ice builds up on my dog ramp. I chisel the ice off.

Ice-melt does not work at temperatures below 10 degrees. In that event, we just wait for the weather to get better. One option you have for stubborn chunks of ice is to use a blowtorch. I have a propane blowtorch that I don't use currently but it's there if I ever need it.

If you live in a heavy snow area, you definitely want a gas-powered snow blower to clear your driveway. You can also hire a plow service to clean you on heavy snow days. Your home is a business now and you cannot have a snowed up driveway. You have to have it clear for clients to come and go safely, without slipping.

In snowy weather, dogs will develop ice balls on their feet when they walk. The hot body temperature will melt the snow that the dog is standing on, and then the ice will reform on the dog's fur as it cools. You will notice a dog is limping when this happens. The best thing to do is check the paw with your hand, and squeeze the Paw gently, to melt the ice with your body temperature.

I personally don't think it's safe to walk dogs in temperatures below 20 degrees. Unless you are training Alaskan huskies, this should not be a problem for you.

If you experience cold weather for too long, your dogs will get a little stir crazy. Dogs need activity in order to feel good. Think of ways to burn off that energy indoors, by tossing the tennis ball around or playing games inside.

ʕ(¯· ᴥ ¯·)ʔ

Laundry

25% of your job as a dog professional is cleaning pee and poop.

Dog sitting is the best job in the world, and you are so lucky that pee and poo keep millions of people from looking at this as a career. If you can't handle pee and poo, this is not the business for you.

Let's talk about the washer and dryer for a moment. The average washer and dryer combo cost $800. And this would be a fancy model, that would not handle the commercial capacity of a dog professional. The average home washes three loads of laundry a week, but the dog professional washes one or two a day. This type of wear and tear on the washer and dryer means that you have to have a stronger machine, that will last longer than a conventional residential unit.

You should search Google for used appliances near you.

Find a used appliance store and check out their washers and dryers. I have a good hook up in my area. I get a washer and dryer for $200 each, and they come with a one-year warranty. These machines were used in a college dormitory for one year, and then sold as used. I have been using them for about four years and I am happy with the machines.

It makes no sense to buy a new washer and dryer from a store, because you will abuse that machine too much, with so many loads. Get a used machine with a good warranty and you will do much better.

When I have a blanket or bed sheet with dog poop on it, I will pick up the dog poop with a plastic grocery bag, and toss it in the trash can, that is actually a small 5 gallon bucket, specifically for dog poop. Then the blanket or sheet goes in my washer machine, with a full load of dog towels and rags. I set the machine to medium duty color setting.

I use a cheap soap powder, for detergent. Please be careful with your detergent use. It seems the trend of detergent manufacturers is to make detergents smell stronger, and clean brighter. But these chemicals and treatments are bad for the dogs' skin.

Dogs get allergies easily from the chemicals in detergents. Go very light on detergents in the laundry. Don't use fabric softeners, that's ridiculous. Don't use the manufacturer's recommendation for detergent, or you will get dogs itching themselves all day. Go as light as possible, to get the clothes clean.

In some cases, you might even consider just washing the load with hot water and no soap at all. Use your own judgment.

When a dog poops on a dog bed, I removed the fitted bed sheet and put it in a locking plastic storage container in the dog area. The latches lock, so the dogs cannot disturb the soiled sheets. When the container is full of dirty laundry, I will take the container to the laundry room for washing.

I keep all the clean laundry in my spare bathroom in the dog area. I use the spare bathroom to fill up the mop bucket, to store the dry dog food, and the store the dog blankets, towels, rags, and bed sheets. I do not fold these blankets or towels, I just keep them in a clean pile on the floor. This actually makes it easier for me to find what I'm looking for. You might think this is crazy, but find whatever works for you.

I always keep a couple of big bath towels and a couple standard size dish rags nearby in the main living room. I need to be ready to deal with any spill or pee right away before it can spread.

Never wash your personal clothes with your dog clothes. Your wife will get mad at you LOL.

6(˘ ∗ ˘)υ

Diarrhea

One of the worst situations you will see as a dog sitter is diarrhea. Diarrhea is so difficult to clean. It is a serious health issue for the dogs and we need to talk about it.

You never want to switch a dog's food dramatically, or you will see diarrhea.

So let's say a dog comes to your home, and he is currently eating grain-free puppy food with "first ingredient" is chicken. If this dog runs out of food, and I can't get the exact same brand, which happens fairly often, I will make sure I get a grain free puppy food with chicken as its first ingredient.

You really want to make sure your dogs are not chewing stuff they aren't supposed to. If a dog eats pieces of plastic, or poisonous plants on the yard, including mushrooms, you will see diarrhea and upset stomach. When you do your daily yard check to pick up poop, you want to make sure nothing unsafe is on the yard.

Be careful what treats you give your dog. Over time I have learned to trust certain treats, and they are usually the mild treats that don't have a powerful flavor, but are very easy on the stomach.

The tastiest treats might be the ones that give them indigestion.

Monitor your treats carefully and if you see any loose stool in the yard, dial the treats back.

Today I had to train a puppy using hot dog slices. That is not my first choice, but the puppy was finicky, and was not interested in traditional 4 calorie treats from a bag.

When a dog has diarrhea, you should notify the owner right away. This keeps them abreast of the news. You will tell the owner how bad the diarrhea is, and you might even suggest a veterinarian visit if you feel it's necessary. I usually wait a couple of days before doing that. If things get bad, and you see bloody stool, or vomiting, or foreign objects in the stool, you will use your best judgment and decide if an emergency veterinarian visit is appropriate.

The best remedy for diarrhea is rest. Give the dog less kibble than usual to ease the stomach. Don't give the dog treats until she regains her health. I have some Pepto-Bismol chewable tablets that I might dip in peanut butter and give to a dog with diarrhea.

You should never ever put a dog or puppy with diarrhea in a crate.

If they poop in close-quarters like the crate, they will stand in the poop, and lay in the poop, and then you will have to bathe the dog, and thoroughly scrub the entire crate.

The best remedy for diarrhea is to put the dog in a small area, like a garage or laundry room. There should be enough room for the dog to poop in one corner of the room, and then move to another corner to sleep. This way you won't have the dog tracking the poop all over the home, and the dog won't have to stand in her own poop.

Obviously, a dog with diarrhea should be taken outside more frequently and encouraged to poop out there.

I wish there was better medicine and treatment for dogs with diarrhea but the truth is it takes time for the stomach to settle down. I have taken many, many dogs to the veterinarian for diarrhea, and they don't do a whole lot for them. They check to make sure it's not viral, or the result of eating something poisonous, and if it's standard typical diarrhea they might give you an antacid or something.

You should never see blood in the stool. You should never see foreign matter like pieces of plastic, and you should never see parasites. Any of these things will require a visit to the veterinarian promptly.

૮(¯· ᴥ ·¯)ა

Dogs In Heat

A female dog will go in heat, starting with her first heat at about 6 months of age. She will stay in heat for about three weeks on average, and she will do this heat cycle about every six to eight months.

The first thing you will notice is small traces of blood on the couch, or the floor, or her dog bed. Her vagina will appear swollen.

It is a really bad idea for you to keep a dog in heat with intact males. No one wants mixed breed puppies, and the owners are not ready to handle a litter of puppies, because they are not breeders. If you allow a dog to get pregnant in your home, that is bad for your reputation as a dog professional.

Don't expect owners to tell you if their dog is in heat.

I know one owner, she seems to bring the dog only when the dog is in heat. She pretends like she did not know her dog is in heat, but I believe she just doesn't want to deal with the blood in her home, so she hires me to deal with it in mine. I'm okay with that because she pays. I think she's taking a big risk, exposing her fertile dog to the unfixed male dogs in my home.

The only method I know that makes any sense is to keep the female separated from all male unfixed dogs. I will usually keep the fertile female in the back room, confined in her own area. She will get yard time by herself or with females. I can't allow her to be bleeding on my furniture.

As soon as you notice a dog in heat, you should notify the owner. This way you're protecting yourself. If the owner doesn't tell you that she has a fertile female, and the dog gets pregnant, that is something she should have shared with you beforehand.

I never ever let dogs dry hump or mount each other.

That is aggressive behavior, sexual behavior, and has no place in my home. Any dogs who are bothering other dogs by mounting, or sexual aggression, or intrusive sniffing, I don't know allow any of that, and the dog will be secluded or given a time out until the behavior is corrected.

In fact, if a male dog is not fixed, and he's too sexually active and disruptive in my home, I will mention it to the owner and there's a good chance I won't watch that dog in the future.

I never use those onesies for dogs, they look like underwear.

Some people will put this on the rear of the dog, to prevent stains on the furniture, and to prevent sex. But my experience has been that dogs are going to find a way to have sex, and they will remove the underwear or diaper. I can't take that risk. I have seen dogs make love through a chain-link fence, so if they can bypass the fence, they can bypass a silly underwear or diaper.

There is also the increased risk of a dog in heat escaping from your yard. The urge to procreate is the strongest urge next to hunger, and dogs frequently escape the yard in order to find sex. Keep a close eye on digging and jumping behavior from a dog in heat, and if you see that, obviously you will limit the yard time and increase the supervision.

ᒪ(⁻ ⋏ ⁻)ᗡ

Patience! Meditation!

This type of work is extremely stressful. The dogs are going to wear you down. You will have to learn how to maintain control, while you are cleaning pee and poo, monitoring puppies, and breaking up rough play. There are scheduling problems, behavior problems, house cleaning problems, and it is a stressful job.

The best advice I could give you as a new dog professional, is to practice patience and meditation.

You did not choose this career because you are greedy. You love dogs. Don't ever let your frustration spill out into your work.

If you walk into a room, and the dogs fear you, you need to back up on the heavy corrections. If the puppies pee when they see you, you are too firm with discipline, and not friendly enough.

You need to find the correct balance, to be effective as a dog professional, and still be loving, compassionate, and trusted by the dogs.

Because this is a 24-hour and seven-day-a-week job, you will have to keep yourself busy at home while you work. I don't waste my time with video games and nonsense. I am an amateur writer in my spare time ,and I have penned 12 books similar to the one you're holding. You can keep yourself busy with activities that allow you to watch the dogs at the same time.

One of the favorite things I love to do, is practice yoga and meditation in the home. I put on some peaceful psybient music, and when I relax, the dogs also relax. I am careful not to step on the dogs in yoga.

You can do whatever you want in your home while you are dog sitting. But I am recommending yoga and meditation, because it really does relax you, and allows you to do your job much better. Meditation reduces your stress levels, and that reduces the stress levels of the dogs you watch. There is a definite connection.

I also suggest that you put on relaxing music whenever you want the group of dogs to slow down and chill out. I love psybient music, but you definitely don't want angry or aggressive music, or the dogs could become agitated.

It is super easy to get frustrated with a puppy or a mischievous dog.

Meditation has taught me to monitor my emotional levels, and when I am stressed, frustrated, or "going dark", I know how to back up, and let myself calm down before proceeding. You need to learn this as well. Otherwise you could lose your cool and injure dog, and that could mean the end of your business.

The skill of a dog professional is his mastery of effective discipline, and the love bond connection with the dog. If you have too much discipline, (or too much love) you are not doing good dog training.

Patience is a super important quality. If you feel like you are more of a prison warden, constantly policing the dogs, and cracking down heavy when they break the rules, you need to adopt a more "caregiver" attitude of compassion, safety, but with more smiles, laughs and fun times.

I cannot judge you or your performance from where I sit. You should look at your group of dogs and assess yourself.

Do these dogs love you? Do they respect you when you give them a command? Do they fear you? Are they being trained correctly? Are the clients happy when the dog returns home? These questions should guide you, so you find that perfect balance between upholding the rules of the house, and loving the dogs with all the love and affection they deserve.

ʖ(ˉ̈ ᴥ ˉ̈)ʋ

This Is An Interactive Book

I truly want you to succeed in your dog sitting and puppy training business. So I'm doing something that I wish someone did for me when I started. I'm including my email address and I'm inviting you to contact me if you have any questions or just wanted chat about dogs in general.

My email address is AlexPuppyTrainer@gmail.com

I invite you to message me anytime, I am probably training puppies right this very minute, and would love to hear from you.

The dog business is not terribly complicated, but I don't want you to stumble around for years, and make the same mistakes I made. Hopefully this book will save you a lot of frustration and expense.

Please feel free to email me anytime, to talk about any dog related subject.

ʖ(ˉ̈ ᴥ ˉ̈)ʋ

More Tips

In this section I'm going to talk about things that are important enough for you to know, but not important enough to deserve their own chapter in this book.

Don't take small breed puppies or toy breeds in the winter months. They will never be able to learn housebreaking in freezing temperatures. You should schedule and postpone tiny breed puppies for the springtime. Trust me, the owner will not housebreak the puppy themselves. You are not losing any business.

Never walk your dogs in temperatures below 20° Fahrenheit. You may think you can handle the cold, but if something goes wrong out there, you're going to have a real crisis on your hands. If a dog gets away from you in freezing temperatures, it could be disastrous. Be smart. Don't walk dogs in freezing temperatures.

You should always have poop bags on you. It is very bad socially to leave dog poop on the sidewalk or street. Your neighbors are always watching you. Don't be a pig. I have 10 poop bags in each of my two back pockets. That way if I run out of bags in one pocket, I have more in the next. When one pocket is empty, I will put one poop bag back in my front pocket, to remind me to replenish my supply. I also have a spare poop bag in my wallet, just in case I got caught super unprepared. You should have the same level of responsibility for picking up your dog poop.

When a dog comes to my home, she will typically have personal property, a leash, maybe some dog bowls, chew toys, tennis balls, and she may come with a favorite teddy bear or plush toy. Whatever the dog arrives with, is going to go into a white grocery plastic bag. I will write the dog's name on it, and put it in the property closet. Of course I would never put the dog's dry kibble in the closet. That goes in the spare bathroom, because dogs can't have access to food. Then when the dog is going home, I simply grab the property bag with her name on it, I grab her dry kibble, which also has her name marked on the bag, and she is ready to go home. If an owner gives you dog treats, you should take a reasonable amount, and put it in a little cookie jar up on a high shelf, to share with the dogs. Don't take more than is reasonable. Always share your treats with everyone, not just the dog whose owner purchased them, that would be unfair. If a dog owner gives you several tennis balls, it is okay to keep one tennis ball for the dogs to play with, and put the others in the property bag to give back to the owner. If the dog has a plush toy, you can never put that out with the dogs, because they will rip it up for sure. Put that in the property bag. If a dog owner gives you several hard rubber chew toys or deer antlers, you should keep one of those, and give the rest back at the end of the stay.

Dogs will take the toys in your home, and drag them outside, in the mud and rain and snow, making them super filthy. It's part of dog behavior, and they all do it. You can't let a dog bring a dirty, filthy, muddy toy from outside into your clean home. So what you want to do, is have a 5 gallon bucket near the back door, near the doggie door. When they bring in a dirty toy, you can toss it in the bucket. When the bucket gets halfway full, you should go outside in the yard, and pick up all the toys that need to be cleaned. If you see a tennis ball that is ripped in half, or a toy that is damaged, throw it away. The rest of the toys will go in the bucket and then you will put them in the washing machine. You don't have to dry them or use soap. Just a good hot water wash is enough.

When you put a puppy or a dog outside in bad weather, you cannot leave them out there for very long. Whether it's raining hard or snowing hard, or you are seeing freezing temperatures, it is very irresponsible to neglect the dogs outside. That said, if you are housebreaking, or giving the dogs a pee break, you have to give them enough time to handle their business. The solution is to use your smartphone. You will use your Google app, just start a timer for 10 minutes or 5 minutes, depending on the weather. This timer will alert you so you can let the dogs back inside.

You want to keep all food behind a closed door. I have used my spare bathroom as a dog food pantry. When a dog comes to my home, I take a big black marker and put her name on her bag of kibble. I make sure the bag is closed and if it is a loose open bag, I roll it up tight and put a heavy towel on the top so it does not unroll and open. This room is free from all insects and odd smells. This room is safe from all curious dogs. Some dogs who are food-obsessed will try very hard to get to food, so you have to protect the food by putting it behind a closed door.

When a puppy is graduating from puppy training, I will prepare a graduation folder. This folder contains a progress report, that covers every step of the training we did together. It's full of helpful advice, and explains in detail what the dog learned with me, and how to keep the progress going when she gets home. I also include the Canine Good Citizen paperwork, that the owner has to mail to the AKC to get the certificate. I use a yellow marker to highlight the areas on the form that the owner needs to fill out herself. The Canine Good Citizen forms come with these attractive blue ribbons. I staple the blue ribbon to the graduation folder, it looks very nice. If you ever have a special dog and you really want to give them special recognition for training, or because they are an exceptionally special client, you should go to a trophy shop, and buy a beautiful plaque with the dog's picture laminated on it, with some beautiful title, like Certified Therapy Dog, or Canine Good Citizen Graduate. Customers really respond well to these plaques, and they could easily stay in the home for decades. Your business name and phone number would be on the back of the plaque, to remind them to call you for future business.

I am guilty of giving dogs human food. It is a powerful motivator and reinforces positive behavior. I feel it is unfair for me to cook eggs and ham in the morning, let the dogs smell it, and then give them nothing. I am very careful about what I give the dogs, I know exactly what they can handle. If I give them meat, it is with no salt, oils or spices. I will give a dog eggs if there is nothing on it. They love peanut butter, and I use peanut butter to give them pill form medication. Most dogs are okay eating bread as a treat. Of course I stay away from the obvious poisons, grapes, raisins and chocolate. Dogs love cheese and milk, but you will get diarrhea if you give them more than just a taste. My personal dogs can handle a small amount of milk every night. I drink 2% milk.

When I give a puppy a munchy stick, I never give them the rawhide pencil-shaped chews, because they could choke on the long piece of rawhide. Munchy sticks are safer, because they break down to small pieces that can easily be digested by a puppy. If you give treats to your dogs, including munchy sticks, you want to make sure you don't see food aggression. If it's a small treat you just hand it out one at a time, never ever throwing it on the floor because they will fight for it. If one dog is being intrusive, while you are giving the treats out, and trying to take it from the other dogs, use your body to block the offending dog. If that doesn't work put that dog in a crate for a time-out.

When you are baby-proofing your home, you want to be very careful about electrical wires. I have all my outlets and surge strips protected, by blocking access to those areas with pillows, 5-gallon buckets, furniture, etc. I make absolutely sure they can't get to the wires. If a puppy or adult dog chews through electrical wires, they could easily kill themselves. I have a number of wires protruding from my laptop and hard drives, in the center of my living room. How can I protect those? I purchased a large rubber hose, approximately 2 inches diameter, and 4 feet long. I sliced this hose vertically, and wrapped it around the wires coming off my laptop. This way if a puppy bites into the hose, it will be a long time before she gets to the live wires inside. Also, I can see marks of teeth on the hose, and I will know that I have a nosy puppy, and I will make sure that puppy stays away from these wires.

I have a lot of "props" in my home. A prop is like a fishing lure, something shiny to attract a mischievous dog. I have a shelf that is the height of a dog's nose, and I have old chewed up things there, like a basket, and an old pottery vase, and a old stack of books. These things are obviously off-limits, as they are on a shelf. I put those there to "tempt" the dog to break the rules, and chew on these things. This way I am not angry when the dog makes the mistake, I will simply correct the dog so she can learn. But if I didn't have these props out, she would start chewing on cell phones, shoes, and valuable things that I really care about. You should put props in your home as well, to teach the dog to respect things that are on a shelf or off-limits. This is all about teaching your dogs boundaries.

I keep a schedule on my laptop, of puppy training arrival and departure dates. I use this puppy schedule to determine when to start a new puppy in training. I don't want to overwhelm myself with 2 new puppies at the same time. I like to stagger the puppies, so that they come every two weeks. This way the first puppy is mostly housebroken and I can focus primarily on the second puppy's behavior. I also have my clipboard, which I keep on my table at all times, this is where I write down the name of every dog who is scheduled to come, with the arrival date, the departure date, and any small notes about the dog. On the first page of the clipboard is my daily activity page, and that consists of dogs who are coming and going today, with their arrival time or approximation, and possibly other notes, like how much the total fee for the stay is. It also has a list of things I want to accomplish today.

I use floor rugs in my home, to allow dogs coming in from the yard to clean their feet a little bit, before they enter the living room area. If it is summer time, I will clean these floor rugs, by taking them outside and spraying them with the garden hose, and letting them sun dry. If it is winter, I have been putting the rugs in my bathtub, and rinsing them down in there. The puppies will often pee or poop on these rugs, and that's okay because that's how they learn. I have several rugs in the laundry room, which is the first room new clients come in through, and those rugs are there for the clients to clean their feet from snow or mud.

When I am doing the daily feedings, I need the dogs to eat quickly. So I use cans of wet dog food, to mix some flavor onto the kibble of each individual dog. My favorite brands of wet dog food is Pedigree Choice Cuts in gravy and Alpo Prime Cuts in gravy. I trust these Brands because they don't give the dogs diarrhea, and by adding a little flavor, they eat the food happily, and we can finish feeding quickly. I spend probably $10 a week on wet dog food, but it's totally worth it because of the convenience of them finishing quickly.

If you experience heavy rains in your area, mud can be a problem. The dogs go outside, and they love mud, but then they'll bring it back inside your home, and cause you great hassles. I like to buy 2 big bales of hay from the local Farm Supply and scatter that on the mud. This creates a thin layer of straw that keeps the dogs feet clean, and soaks up a lot of the rainwater.

I used two different types of ice-melt for snowy days. On my driveway, I use the standard rock salt, because it's more reliable and it does a better job. But inside my home, I use the pet-friendly ice-melt for the doggie ramp, near the doggie door. I do this because it's gentler on the paws of the dog. I also have a ice chipping tool that looks like a hoe, and that is used to keep ice from building up on the dog ramp.

When you have freezing weather, you will experience frozen piles of dog poop in your yard. They are very hard to clean because they are frozen to the ground. What I like to do is I use a shovel flat nose, and I dig the poop and flick it to the edge of the fence. This way the dogs won't walk in it, and I can pick it up when the weather is better. It is really easy to walk along the line of the fence and pick up piles of poop, that I had put there earlier, when the weather was freezing. When the poop thaws, it becomes soft again, so you want to flick it to the edge of the fence so that dogs can't walk in it.

Be careful when you are cleaning the dog dishes. Don't use heavy soaps because dogs are very sensitive to that stuff. Also, when you are cleaning the house, make sure you don't allow any Lysol or cleaning products to contaminate the drinking water bowls, or the dog food bowls. When I want to clean the dog dishes, I will usually just soak them in the sink until the next meal. This will loosen all the crusted on food. I only use stainless steel bowls because they are the best. My stainless steel bowls can be soaked for hours and then easily wiped clean.

When you have a fenced yard, dogs will try to dig near the fence. This is bad. You can prevent this by buying a bunch of paving stones, roughly 2 inches thick, and 1 foot square diameter. Put these paving stones along the edge of your fence on the inside line. Now the dog cannot dig near the fence, because he can't dig through a concrete block.

If you have a finicky dog, who doesn't respond to the wet dog food, or traditional treats, I have a lot of luck with grated cheese. I put a little grated cheese on top of the dog food, it gives it an interesting flavor, and the dogs usually eat.

You should keep some children's Benadryl in your medicine cabinet, in case a dog has a serious allergy. If a dog gets stung by a bee, or as an allergic reaction to food, you may need to administer a children's Benadryl to reduce inflammation. You should always get permission before giving medicine to a dog. The exception is if you feel the dog is going to die without the medicine. Use your best judgment, but remember that you are not a veterinarian, so always err on the side of good judgment.

I also keep Pepto-Bismol tablets, the chewable kind, in my medical supply kit. This is for dogs with diarrhea. What I will do is dip the Pepto-Bismol chewable in peanut butter, and give it to the dog. This usually helps calm the stomach.

If you're giving medicine of any kind to a dog, your best bet is to put the pill in a gob of peanut butter and give it to the dog. I will put my two fingers in the peanut butter jar, then put the pill in the middle of the Gob of peanut butter, and then come up to the dog, and wipe it into his mouth, so that it's stuck to the roof of his mouth. Peanut butter is the best way to get a dog to take his pill.

When you get up in the middle of the night, to give the dogs a pee break, you don't have time to get dressed, and put your fancy coat and hat on. Dogs don't give you that luxury. If you are training puppies for housebreaking, the second that you wake up and make noise, the dog will realize he has to pee, and could possibly pee in the crate while you are getting your clothes on. I have a midnight robe, and slip-on shoes, that I keep near my bed. As soon as I hear a commotion downstairs, I get up like a firefighter out of my bed, I throw on that bathrobe on, and the slip-on shoes, and I'm ready to go downstairs and deal with things, like an unexpected poo or pee accident, or a restless dog, or something of that nature. Notice I said slip-on shoes. Don't use flip-flops or slippers because that is a bad idea. You need actual shoes, but you need shoes that can go on your feet very quickly, like slip-ons or Crocs.

ᕙ(͡° ͜ʖ ͡°)ᕗ

Marketing

Primary Marketing Strategy

Marketing is such a big subject that I will break down different types of marketing efforts in smaller sections.

I believe that marketing is the lifeblood of any small business. I would rather be an expert marketer and an average dog trainer, than being an expert dog trainer and an average marketer. It's that important.

Let's start with the biggest marketing ally you can have as a dog sitter: Rover.com.

Rover.com makes it easy for a dog sitter to advertise locally, using their website. Potential clients can check your availability, see pictures of your home, read reviews from past clients, see your daily rate, and even message you with any questions.

Rover.com is huge and you should definitely sign up for it. The only drawback is they charge 20% of all business done through the site. So if you have a client that does business through Rover for 5 years, you will be paying five years of a 20% service fee to Rover.

Rover insures the stay booked through its site. They handle all the credit card payments from the client in advance, and they send you payment by PayPal. Rover is like an Uber for dog sitting.

I am no longer on Rover, but that's because I have established my own reliable clients, and my Facebook posts get enough attention for me to not need Rover. But you will definitely want to use Rover. It could easily be 25 to 50% of all your dog sitting business.

To be accepted by Rover, you will have to pass an interview by phone. They will do a background check and they will ask for pictures of your home and your experience, etc.

When you send a client a picture of a dog on Rover, it becomes a public photo that any viewers of the website can see.

I think Rover is so important that it will have its own subsection later in the book.

Another internet marketing technique I use is posting paid ads on Facebook. This costs me much less than my Rover service fee.

When I want to put an ad on Facebook for dog sitting or puppy training, I will go on Reddit, and search for the cutest puppies in the whole world. This collection of awesome puppy pictures will be used in my Facebook ad, to make ladies heart melt. These puppies have a tremendous Aww Factor. For me, this is way more cost-effective marketing then Rover. But Rover is still vital, and is your number one resource when you are a new sitter.

Do not waste your time on Craigslist. Only creepers and broke people go on Craigslist. Trust me, you will pay for the ad, $10 each, and you will not get any calls. I hate to be honest about Craigslist, because I used to really love the website, but it has gone to trash in the last few years, and it's completely worthless now.

Don't waste your time on thumbtack.com. You will pay for leads that are fake or not very solid. Just like Craigslist, Thumbtack needs to clean up their act.

I am a big fan of guerrilla marketing. My personal vehicle has a 2-foot by 3-foot vinyl advertisement on the rear window, with my business name, phone number, brief description of services, and a picture of an adorable puppy.

I live in a small farm town, and once a year we have a big parade. Everyone brings their dog to the parade, and I walk with my dogs, up and down the sidewalk of the parade, handing out business cards to dogs that look friendly.

I have my business cards at several locations in the city. At the hardware store, at the local diners, and the coffee house, I thumbtack my cards to the post-it board. But my biggest success with business cards is having them at the veterinarian, the groomer, and the local pet stores.

My local pet food store allows me to put a very large sign, 3 foot by 2 foot inside, his pet store. That helps a lot.

Like I said, my strength in marketing is posting incredibly cute videos of puppies being trained, and the cute things that puppies do, and posting my dogs running off-leash through forests and meadows. By posting frequently on Facebook, I am using the natural love that people have for dogs and puppies, to support my strong marketing. Nobody wants to see my ugly face on a marketing promotion, they would rather see a cute girl, holding a beautiful, adorable puppy.

Another marketing strategy I have is, whenever I receive a puppy in my home, I ask the owners for the phone number to the breeder. Then I contact the breeder, and tell him that I am training one of his puppies. I offer to make him a deal, whereby we both can profit handsomely. For every client he refers to me for puppy boot camp, I will give him a referral fee of $100. This is huge for the breeder. So the breeder will constantly be telling his clients about my puppy training. In fact some breeders will even put a flyer or brochure about my training into their puppy package. Again, this is a huge marketing strategy.

One marketing strategy I use is, to have really good public relations and image in my neighborhood. I am often posting profiles of dogs who are in need of adoption on my Facebook. This helps me a lot.

Another marketing technique I use is, creating an intensely positive experience with each client.

This is so important that it will be in its own subsection. But I will briefly say that I treat each dog as if they are super special. I am constantly sending pictures of the dog having fun to the owner, whether it's a training puppy, or a dog vacation sitting. By always making comments like, "I love your dog..." "Your dog is wonderful..." "Your dog behaved perfectly", "I hope I get to see your dog again soon", "Your dog is so cute!" This may sound insincere to you, but I'm being totally sincere. I really do love these dogs. And I want the client to know that. Dogs are super special to me and they are the focus of my life at this point, and so I'm not exaggerating when I say that I love them, and that they are special, each one of them. I think that the genuine feeling I have for dogs, shines through the "schmoozing".

To be honest, I have such strong marketing, that paid advertising for the most part does not make sense right now. That is because I have a limited amount of space in the home. The maximum number of dogs I feel comfortable with his 10. Sometimes, on Christmas or Thanksgiving or spring break, that number could go to 13. That's a lot of dogs to manage!

So please remember that! You have a limited number of available spaces in your home. Rover won't even allow you to book more than five dogs in your home on one day.

When a holiday approaches, you're going to get a ton of calls, but your priority is to your regular clients. So the wise dog sitter will message his favorite clients, and ask them if they need a sitter for the holiday upcoming. This way you don't have to do the awkward phone call of declining a regular client, because they waited to the last minute to book you on a holiday. This also makes your regular clients feel special, because you offered them the reservation first.

Another marketing strategy I do is, I train therapy dogs. This will be covered in a subsection of the book because it deserves its own space.

There is a nursing home in my community that is very large, with over 1,000 residents. When I bring the therapy dogs for a visit, I have business cards in my pocket, and when a nurse pets the dogs I ask her, "Do you have a dog?" If she says yes, I hand her my card and tell her that I'm a dog sitter. I can't even count how many clients I got with this simple technique.

A large part of your marketing is going to be how clean your home is, how quiet and poop free your place is, and the public image you develop. Another great thing about Rover is that you can view the rates, services, and reviews of your local competition. So I know exactly how much money I should charge for my services, and Rover helps me stay familiar with my local competition.

I have an edge in my marketing, because I do more than the regular sitters. I do not charge for free daily walks. And I am sure to tell new clients that. I also have very flexible pick-up and drop-off times. All the client has to do is tell me, the day before, what time they're going to arrive, so that I can be ready for them. I try my hardest to make myself available for them, and that is an edge over a typical kennel, who has one or two fix drop off times, with few exceptions.

Perhaps my biggest marketing tool, is the way the dogs leave my home, and arrive. These dogs have to like being at my home. At the very minimum they cannot dislike my home. If a client is driving to my home and the dog is nervous, and does not want to go inside my home, that's a bad image, and bad marketing, and you might lose that client. You want to be firm with the rules of the house, while the dog is here, for safety and sanity. But you also want the dog to have a very pleasant experience. Spend time with the dog, bond with the dog, and make the dog feel comfortable, safe, and happy.

In my local area, I have been in the newspaper twice for dog training. The newspaper is a dying medium, like Craigslist. Even though I had a big splash in the newspaper I did not get any business from that, and so I would not recommend it as a marketing tool.

I use Google My Business a lot. I post there once a week, for free, and when someone uses Google Maps, they see my business on the map. I come up in search listings, and because it's free, it doesn't have to bring a lot of clients to be worth the effort of renewing the post each week or two.

When you walk your dogs, you are going to meet your neighbors, who are also walking their dogs. Friendships should ensue. You have a common love of dogs, and you are neighbors, so reach out and be friendly. Some of my clients do business with me, because friends tell friends, who tell other friends, and this is huge for marketing your business. You should have business cards in your pocket ready to hand out. I keep mine in a metal card case, so they don't get wrinkled.

ᘓ(ˉ· ᴥ ˉ·)ᘎ

Taking Photos and Videos

I am constantly using my Android phone, to take videos and still photos of the dogs. This is a huge part of my customer service, and my marketing. As soon as a dog gets to my home, and the owner leaves, I feel it is important for me to take a picture of the dog, looking comfortable and relaxed, in the home or in the yard. This will ease the clients' concerns, and let her enjoy her vacation or business trip without worrying. This is part of my customer service, and the reason why clients return year after year.

Another reason I'm taking photos and especially videos, is to post them on Facebook and YouTube. Dogs are naturally photogenic. They are cute, they are impressive physical animals, and they're always doing something interesting. Over the years I've learned how to take excellent photos and videos.

Every morning when I walk the dogs, I take a picture of them on their leash as we walk, either one dog at a time or with multiple dogs. I will text message this picture to the owner, so she knows the dog is getting daily walks. If I am walking the dogs before 9 a.m., I will schedule the message for after 9 a.m., because I don't want to be waking anyone up. If it's Sunday morning I will schedule the message for after 10 am.

I especially love to take videos of the puppies when they are being trained. I post these puppy training videos on my Facebook, and people melt, because the puppies are so cute, smart, and likable This is good for business.

Whenever asks me for my puppy training credentials, I usually refer them to the 500+ videos I posted on Facebook and YouTube, of me training puppies. If they ask for more proof, I feel they are not worth the bother. Don't let people bug you with requests for tax information, training credentials, and nonsense like that. Experience tells me that my clients don't ask for stuff like that, only strangers pretending to be interested clients.

I also take lots of photos that the nursing home, when I bring a therapy dog for training. I post these photos of the dog being petted, making new friends at the retirement home, and people see that on Facebook. While therapy dogs are not a huge part of my business, totaling roughly $1,000 a year so, it is great public relations, and it is a lot of fun.

When you are taking a picture of a dog, sometimes it's best to kneel down at their face level.

I have 2 cameras on my camera phone. The first is the standard one that comes with the phone. I set it so I can double-click my button, super fast, and take a picture. I don't have to unlock my phone or open it. This helps me catch a special moment easier than if I had to unlock my phone and open the app.

I have another camera app that I use for superior pictures. But this app does not allow me the quick-opening feature. So I use this one for portraits. It has great lighting, and the shutter speed is faster, so I don't get the blurry shots as much.

To be honest, most of the pictures that I post on advertisements are not actually dogs in my home. I go on Reddit, and I search for puppy photos from all over the world. I select puppy photos that already have tens of thousands of likes, so I know these are superior photos. I use these pictures in advertisements, and that's why my ads really do touch a person in their heart.

I never send a video of a dog directly to my client, because that would use up all their data bandwidth on their phone. My cell phone has unlimited data, but that doesn't mean everyone else's does.

So my method is, I will upload the video to YouTube, and then copy the link and just send them the link. They can decide if they want to use it, or forward it to their home computer, or use it when they have public Wi-Fi. I will also upload the video to Facebook if it's interesting.

ᕦ(ˉ ᴥ ˉ)ᕤ

Community Partners

Community Partners are essential to good marketing and public relations. I'm going to tell you about my special relationships, and I encourage you to develop similar relationships in your community, for a strong and positive presence in your area.

First let's start with breeders. Since you are a puppy trainer, you obviously want to know all the active puppy breeders in your area. How would you find out who is actively breeding puppies near you?

The easiest way is whenever a puppy books with you for puppy training, you simply ask the owner for the phone number of the breeder. Explain to them that you want to offer the breeder a special deal on puppy training referrals.

The referral deal I'm speaking of is: I will offer any breeder a $100 referral fee for any paying client they refer to me, for the $600 puppy training boot camp. I will print out brochures and flyers, so they can include it in the puppy package when they sell the puppies.

It's hard to calculate how effective this marketing strategy has been for me. Tens of thousands of dollars in referrals have come from the simple technique. So for every puppy that comes to your home, you should ask the client for the contact information of the breeder.

I recommend you make friends with many breeders. You need to become an expert in dogs, and breeder friends can help you with that. With breeders as friends, you can always text one of them, and ask a question, about a sick dog or puppy, and get a professional answer.

I also make friends with the veterinarians in my area. Or to be more specific, I make friends with the veterinary assistants who run the front desk. These are the girls that I see every time I bring my dogs, and I know them on a first-name basis. We are friends. They let me put my business cards on their desk, in a prominent place, and when they are asked about puppy training or dog sitting, they recommend me.

Sometimes the veterinarian will teach puppy classes. So will a pet store. I don't see these people as my competition. That's because they don't cover housebreaking, and they don't do an in-house puppy boot camp like I do. So if someone does not want my type of training, and they just want the classes, I will refer them to one of my puppy training friends, who does the hourly classes, once a week.

I am friends with the local pet food store. The owner lets me put a 3ft by 3ft vinyl sign in his shop, advertising my services. This is a real good friend, and I want to always cultivate that relationship, by buying food there instead of the grocery store, and by taking an interest in how his business is doing. That's what friends do.

I have a special relationship with the local nursing home. It is a Masonic home and it houses over 1000 seniors. Many of the nurses there are my clients. I bring the therapy dogs into the nursing home for therapy dog visits, and whenever the nurse pets the dog, I ask her if she has a dog. If she says yes, I hand her my business card.

Without my business relationship with the nursing home, therapy dog visits would be difficult. So I want to cultivate and strengthen this relationship, because it translates into real money for me.

Because I am an AKC certified trainer, and I'm the only one in this area, I get a lot of calls for puppy training. I do not do hourly classes under no circumstances. I'm too busy and that's just not my style of training.

Because I am an AKC certified trainer, if someone else wants to train their dog, I would charge $25 just to evaluate the dog, and pass them for the Canine Good Citizen Award. Usually I will ask the owner to videotape his dog, doing all of the commands, and then send me the videos, by email, text, or a link. This way I have video evidence that the dog can perform the commands required. This is more than is required by AKC. And this way the owner doesn't have to pay for training, if the dog is already trained well.

Everyday when I walk the dogs, I follow one of maybe 4 paths. So of course I'm going to see the same dog owners each day along my route.

I have cultivated many special friendships with the neighbors and their dogs. This is a powerful marketing tool, and it's also a great way to live, making friends with your neighbors and their dogs. I can't count how many referrals I got from friendly neighbors, who told other people about my service.

When I'm walking the dogs along the downtown area, I am passing butcher shops, coffee houses, thrift stores, and every other type of downtown business. The people know me and I know them, because my default mode is friendly and professional.

I am a naturally happy person, and I believe that good marketing requires a friendly face, a warm smile, and a positive attitude. If you don't have those things you need to develop them. Marketing is everything, and a person who has a sour face, or does not greet people well, or does not personally like people, that person is at a huge disadvantage in business.

I am friends with the local dog catcher or animal control officer. If I need help catching a stray dog or a dog that escaped from me, I want to rely on the friendship with the animal control officer. The animal control officer in my area helps me re-home dogs as well. So there is a special connection there. We both love dogs. You should be friendly with your animal control officer and work towards making a positive relationship there.

Groomers are another way you can make money in this business. I personally do not do grooming, but if you have the skill and inclination I say go for it. What I do is, if a dog is muddy, with dirty long hair, or fibers and thorns stuck in their hair, I will suggest to the owner that I take the dog to the groomer during the vacation stay. I will charge whatever the groomer charges, usually $40 plus $25 for my time and gas.

Yet another way to make money, if you are inclined to do it, is to offer drop-off and pick-up of dogs that live far away from you. A couple of my clients are willing to travel over a hundred miles to use me as a dog sitter. But I don't feel like that's fair to them, so I offer to meet them halfway. I can't always do this. It depends on how busy I am. But I like to help them when I can, and I just add the gas and time cost to the bill for a travel expense.

I have spoken in front of the 4-H club regarding therapy dogs and puppies, and while this may not be a huge business opportunity, all the parents of the 4-H girls are animal lovers, and it just makes for good community relations.

You are going to cultivate a healthy and positive relationship with the people in your community, and you will fight hard to protect that image. Don't lose your cool on one stupid customer, and then have a bad review following you for the next 5 Years. Be smart.

ʕ(͡° ͜ʖ ͡°)ʋ

Facebook

Facebook is a huge part of social media, and therefore it is a huge part of my business.

The first thing I want to say about Facebook, is my ads are FREE here!

That's because you don't have to "boost" your post, to reach a lot of people in your local area. You can now make a "special offer", and Facebook doesn't charge for posts that offer some sort of discount. So, my favorite discount is "20% Off New Clients' First Stay".

Next, let's talk about your effective service area. If you are posting a puppy training ad, your service area is 100 miles radius around your home. If you are posting a dog sitting ad, the range is 50 miles radius. This is because very few people are willing to drive more than 50 miles to get to the dog sitter.

Every single time I do a therapy dog visit to a nursing home, I take pictures of the dogs being petted by nurses and seniors, and I post that on my therapy dog Facebook page. Then I share that post with my dog sitting page. This way I let all my clients know that I do therapy dog training.

You have the good blessing that your business is dogs, and dogs are very photogenic and appealing. People love dogs, and some people love dogs more than anything!

Use that to your advantage. No one wants to see a picture of your face unless you are a celebrity, but your face next to a cute puppy, is all of a sudden very interesting. You want to show your face smiling, and bonding with the dogs and puppies, as this produces an Aww Factor among your clients.

Once a week I will post a puppy training video, where the puppy is performing the basic commands, looking cute. This link is shared on Facebook and on YouTube. I send the YouTube link to the client. I get approximately 50 to 150 likes for every puppy training post.

If you are walking multiple dogs on a leash, or if you are taking the dogs to a very special place, like a forest or a dog park, that is a good time to video the event and share it with your friends on Facebook.

If I am out in the fenced yard, I am throwing the tennis ball back and forth with the dogs, I like to share that special playtime with the people of Facebook.

I own a GoPro camera, but it's too complicated. I now take my puppy training videos using a police-style body cam. This gives me superior video and audio, and it clips to my belt, at the buckle, so both my hands are free. I like to clip it on my belt, because the dog is the star of the video, and he's much lower to the ground.

On the rare occasions when I feel I should do some advertising, either because my puppy training schedule is light, or my dog sitting business needs a little boost, I will go on Reddit, and search in the "Aww" subgroup, for the most popular photos of puppies. I am not claiming anywhere that these puppies are being watched by me. I am just sharing extremely adorable photos of puppies with my Facebook friends. I will use these photos in a Facebook ad, describing my puppy training program, or my dog sitting.

I don't want people to drive very far to use my business. So I want to saturate my local area with my advertising campaign. For that reason I select my viewing audience for my Facebook ad like this: I don't want to advertise more than 50 miles away from my home, for dog sitting, or more than 100 miles for puppy training. I only want people between 18 and 65 to see my ad. And I want people to have some connection with dogs, so I will use keywords in my ad, like dog training, puppies, dog parks, dog groomer, Etc.

Facebook ads are affordable and effective. Try the discount offer first, because it's free, and if you need more business, you can simply boost the ad for $20.

About once a month, I will re-home a dog. I sometimes find a stray dog in my neighborhood, or someone will tell me they can no longer care for a dog, and ask me to help them find the dog a new home. When this happens, I will post something on Facebook, looking for a forever home for the dog. This makes me look like a hero to my neighbors! And finding a dog a loving home really does make me feel super good inside. This not only helps the dog find a loving forever home, it cement and image in the mind of the public, that I really do care about dogs and that I am a good person with compassion for dogs. Great marketing, and great human kindness!

I get a ton of likes and shares and comments when I post a paid ad on Facebook. However, I've been doing this a long time, and I don't expect a surge in business, just because I put an ad up. The reality is, people only need my service when they have a new puppy, or are planning a business trip or vacation. So my marketing has to coincide with a person's actual need for these services.

You should join Facebook groups in your local area, that can increase your exposure to your neighbors' Facebook feeds. Joining neighborhood groups, local activity groups, these are ways to increase your Facebook presence locally.

I do not have my "review" button turned on my Facebook page.

Anyone can say something rude or untrue on a review, even if they never used your business. Sometimes, I will get animal activists, who should be friends with me, but instead they attack me for using prong collars, or the rare electric collar in my training.

Some other activists resent the fact that I do not accept pit bulls in my home. So they will troll me, and give me bad reviews for refusing to work with pit bulls. For this reason I have turned off my reviews. Use your own judgment on this matter. My recommendation is that because you are a new business, you should turn your reviews on, and ask all your friends, family, and favorite clients to give you a good review. Once you have built your business up, there will come a time where you don't really need the reviews anymore and you can decide whether to keep them or turn them off.

I am a busy person, so I don't have time to be everybody's friend on Facebook. For that reason, if a client sent me a friend request, I decline it. I want people to like my Facebook page, but I don't want to be inundated with pictures and posts of their status update or pictures of their vacation.

I explain to my clients that they are super valuable to me, but the Facebook friend request is a real time-drain. I am not a boomer, I am not retired, so I don't have time to respond to all the posts from people in my area.

If you have spent enough time on Facebook, you will soon realize that the site is not all it could be. I look forward to the day when Facebook is replaced with a better site.

I recommend posting many, many, many, videos and pictures, of dogs doing interesting things, on your Facebook page and YouTube channel. As a new dog trainer, you want to quickly establish your credentials as an expert. Having a few hundred videos on your Facebook page more than proves your love for dogs, and your professionalism. Anyone who asks for more proof than this, is just not a good client for you to pursue.

ᕙ(ﾟ▽ﾟ)ᕗ

Rover.com

Rover.com is your greatest single business partner as a dog sitter.

You can go from knowing almost nothing about dog sitting, to becoming a paid professional, simply by using Rover.com correctly. When I first started dog sitting, the things I learned from Rover were priceless.

You will start by making a profile on Rover. There is a brief interview process, where someone from Rover will do a phone interview, and a simple background check.

When you design your profile for Rover, as a dog sitter, you will select the best pictures of you working with dogs, pictures of your home, and a description of the care you provide. You can mention your experience, your love for dogs, your availability, and things like that.

Dog owners who are looking for a sitter will visit Rover, they will type in their zip code, and your profile will show up. They will see your reviews from previous Rover clients, they will see your availability for certain dates, they will see any restrictions you have as to number of dogs, or breed of dogs, etc. They will see your daily rate.

If a dog owner has any questions for you, she can message you directly through the website. You are obligated to return any messages promptly. You will get a Rover email, text message, and they will bug you if you are late in returning calls. There is a computer algorithm that will make sure that customer messages are returned quickly, otherwise the message could go to another sitter.

When you and a dog owner agree on that vacation stay, Rover will charge the owner's credit card and the stay will show up on your Rover calendar. The maximum dogs you can watch for Rover is 5, but you can watch another five on your own. That is not against the rules.

You are supposed to share photos of the Rover dogs daily, and those pictures show up as public photos on the Rover site. This is standard practice for me anyway. Everyday I send clients pictures of their dog, usually 3 pictures a day.

Rover offers insurance on their vacation stays, but it does not cover anything except gross negligence on the part of the sitter.

Rover takes 20% of the money. I think this is worth it if you are a new sitter, but I have been doing it for a while so I don't need to do Rover, and lose 20% of my income. But if things ever got slow, and I felt I could use a boost, I certainly haven't forgotten about Rover.

If you are a new sitter on Rover, I recommend you boost your activity by asking friends and family to book you through the site. They can also give you great reviews, which will boost your visibility.

Make yourself highly available on the weekly schedule, and you will do well in any area. If you have very limited days or hours, you may not get much business.

Rover has a toll free hotline that both dog owners and dog sitters can call if they have any issues. A customer service agent will walk them through whatever problems arise.

Whether you use Rover or not, it is a fundamental pillar of the dog sitting business. For example, I can go on Rover right now, and determine what the daily dog sitting rate is for my area. I can also see the profile of all the dog sitters around me, and that is huge for marketing and assessing my competition.

ᘛ(ˉ・ ⚶ ˉ)ʋ

Reviews

Reviews are super important to a new dog business. You want to collect reviews for both dog sitting and puppy training.

When someone asks me for reviews, I have some screen shots saved on my computer, of sparkling reviews I received in the past. I collect these reviews, and save them in a folder. I immediately email or text them the images of the reviews.

The more reviews you get on Facebook or Rover, the more business you will get.

Let's talk about Facebook first.

When you start your Facebook page for your dog business, you can decide if you want a separate page for puppy training, and a separate page for dog sitting. I personally describe both services on the same dog sitting Facebook page. I have a separate page for therapy dogs. Whenever I post something on therapy dogs, I share the link to my dog sitting page.

The Facebook reviews are super important, so do your best to keep your reviews positive and perfect. I personally only ask certain clients to give me a review, because I want to make absolutely sure they're not going to give me a four out of five. Maybe they think this is okay, but I don't want to see a number four out of five on my reviews.

Any friends or family that have ever let you watch their dog, for even a few hours, can give you a review on Facebook. If you had a pet cat or dog as a child, you can ask your mother and father to give you reviews about how you cared for your animals on Facebook.

You should have a ton of positive reviews. I am one of those people that look at reviews before I purchase things. If I see very few reviews, or negative reviews, I lose respect for that business, because I feel like they are clueless as to how to manage their social media, and their reviews. So I feel like if they neglect their social media presence, by ignoring the bad reviews, I wonder what else they might be neglecting in their business.

Having bad reviews is kinda like a restaurant with super-dirty windows. If they can't clean the windows, they may not be cleaning the kitchen either. Reviews help me avoid doing business with shady people.

When someone gives you a review, and it's negative, you should reply to their comment, and explain your side of things. Sometimes you can turn a bad review into a good one, simply by defending yourself, and explaining your situation clearly so people understand what really happened. If you reply politely, offering to fix the problem or remedy the complaint, people will actually like your business more.

Rover reviews are even more important than Facebook. Rover will highlight your profile if you have more positive reviews than other sitters.

Your reviews, your pictures that you upload, and your profile description of services, all combine in a complex chemistry, to create a favorable impression to the prospects on Rover. You need to actively maintain your profile image on Rover.

I recommend that you save your Facebook review link on your smartphone, and whenever you meet someone who can give you a favorable review, text them the link. This way you are always ready, when someone says something positive about your business, to thank them and ask them to give you a good review.

6(˙ ⋅ ˙)ʋ

AKC Canine Good Citizen Evaluator

My primary qualification and credential for puppy training is my AKC Canine Good Citizen evaluator status.

When I tell someone that I am an AKC certified trainer, there really is no higher credential in this industry.

If anyone asks for more credentials or qualification than that, I will kindly refer them to the 500 videos I have posted online, that show me training puppies. That is the extent at which I am willing to bend over and show someone why I'm a great trainer. I believe my reputation speaks for itself, and I won't make a huge effort to convince someone that I am right for them. What they will usually discover is that when I blow them off, there are no other trainers the offer what I am offering, chiefly housebreaking and board-and-train boot camp, and they will call me back.

So I recommend you become an AKC trainer as soon as possible. You don't need any other credentials, but you do need this one.

To become an AKC Canine Good Citizen approved evaluator, you must have 2 years of experience working with owners and their dogs, and you must be 18 years or older. You pay a $100 application fee and you're in.

How do you prove that you have 2 years of experience working with dogs?

Well, the easiest way is to start a Facebook page for your dog business. You should stop reading this book right now, and go start your dog training Facebook page if you haven't already done so.

You might be wondering why I don't train adult dogs. The reason is simple. The longer a dog has a behavior problem, the longer it takes to correct the bad habit. I did adult dog training, and my success rate was not good. Aggressive, destructive dogs are super difficult to train, and when I failed, the dog often got put down, for being so aggressive. I hate that feeling, and I hate failing, so I focus chiefly on puppies, because they have no bad habits, no history, and my success is near 100%.

Another reason you don't want to train adult dogs in your home is, they require more physical "spanking", and this creates a bad mood in my home. The more I behave like a disciplinarian, instead of a cheerful friend, the less the dogs trust me.

Back to becoming an AKC Certified Trainer...

Let's say that two years ago, you watched a dog, and you did a little training with the dog. If you have a video or photo of that, you can literally backdate a post, going Back 2 years, on your new Facebook page, and describe your interaction with the dog.

If you have pictures of any dogs that you raised as a child, post those on your Facebook page, and backdate them.

Your Facebook page will have an area where you can describe your experience and services. It is called "Our Story". You should mention in this section how long you have been working with dogs, how many dogs you have watched or cared for throughout your life, and why you decided to get into the dog business.

This Facebook page that I'm describing above, should satisfy the 2-year requirement by the AKC. It did for me.

As an AKC trainer, I train puppies for the Canine Good Citizen Award. I don't spend any time with any other training certificates, because there's not much demand for them.

I spend about $20 every six months, ordering Canine Good Citizen certificate forms from the AKC. For a pack of 20, they charge $20.

When a puppy graduates from puppy boot camp, I fill out the AKC CGC form, and I put that in her graduation folder, to give to the client.

If you have a purebred dog, the Canine Good Citizen Award will attach itself to the dog's AKC history. AKC keeps track of the genealogy of purebreds, awards like the CGC, and other dog-related data, like winning awards and titles.

I have also evaluated dogs that I did not personally train.

You can make a little money doing this. So, when someone wants me to evaluate their dog, but for whatever reason they don't hire me to train the dog, I simply ask them the video their dog, doing the basic commands, that are required under CGC guidelines. When they text or email me the videos of the dog performing the commands, I will fill out the CGC form and give it to them, for a $25 service fee.

I do not use AKC for their therapy dog certificates.

AKC wants 50 facility visits before they grant a therapy dog certificate! They also have many difficult requirements for therapy dog evaluators. For these reasons, I simply certify my therapy dogs under my personal dog sitting business. The client receives a beautiful rosewood trophy plaque, with the dogs picture laminated and sealed in plastic, and her name, with the title "Certified Therapy Dog". This looks a whole lot better than the AKC cheap paper certificate.

When I purchase the CGC forms from the AKC, they come with 20 blue ribbons that are kind of cool. I like to staple them to the graduation folder on the outside, as it makes it look more professional.

ᘓ(¯· ᴥ ¯·)ʋ

CGC Dog Requirements

The Canine Good Citizen test is the only one I deal with, because I specialize in puppies.

There are several other agility and skill tests that the AKC provides, which you can earn money from, by offering to the public. I would recommend that you don't get distracted by some of those fancy tests for advanced agility and a special trick dog titles. Focus on puppy training, and don't get derailed by specialty training. Nobody ever asked me for the specialty training, but people ask me every day for puppy training.

The dog has to pass 10 steps to pass the CGC test.

The dog needs to except a friendly stranger, she needs to sit politely, and allow herself to be petted.

She should be able to walk on a loose leash, through a crowd of people.

And she should be able to sit, stay, come , and go down on command.

The dog should be socially friendly with another dog, and not react poorly to distractions. The dog should accept a temporary separation from her owner.

My training program for puppies is based on this exam. I teach *Sit, Stay, Come, Down*, and *No*. I teach the dog to walk on the leash correctly, and to be friendly with other dogs. I teach the dog not to whine when I leave the room.

As you can see, housebreaking is not a requirement for passing the Canine Good Citizen test. But housebreaking is the number one reason people will call you for puppy training.

To become a master in the dog business, you need to master housebreaking. It's the most difficult part of the training, so if you master it, you can master everything.

You can actually advertise your puppy training services on Rover, and on the AKC website. I don't do this, because I have all the business I need, but if you need to boost your puppy training, this could be the way.

ᘒ(ﾟ ▴ ﾟ)ʊ

Client Relations

I like to call client relations "schmoozing", but not in a disrespectful way.

I want my clients to feel good about their decision to leave their dog in my care. These are some of my secrets.

When a dog first arrives at my home, I want to send a picture of the dog, relaxed and comfortable, in the first 20 minutes. This is because the client is most worried when they drop off the dog, and if I can send a picture showing the dog is comfortable, the client will relax. The client will be able to focus on her vacation, and have fun without the distraction of worrying about her dog.

Whenever you see a dog doing something cute, whip out your phone and take a picture. Send this to the owner. This is Schmoozing 101.

When a client messages me and asks me if I am available to watch her dog on a certain day, this is my standard reply: "Yes, definitely! I love Buster, he is such a happy dog. See you Sunday morning."

Obviously I won't send the exact same text a second time, because that is insincere. But the idea is always there, to make the client feel good about deciding to hire me as a sitter.

If the dog is old or sick, it's super important to message the client frequently about the dog's condition. Take pictures of the dog eating dinner, and take pictures of you petting the dog. This relieves a lot of the owner's anxiety.

Sometimes I will send a message to the owner, praising the dog's personality. I will say, "Buster is such a cool dog! He has such an awesome personality. I am really growing close to Buster." Messages like these, combined with fun, happy, cheerful photographs, do so much to cement the trust and the bond between the dog, the owner, and the sitter.

If a dog is misbehaving, you have to gently inform the client, so as not to upset them. Describe the dog as wild, not a bad dog. Many times a young dog or puppy will come to your home, and the owner will worry that the puppy is too hyper and crazy, and might annoy you as the sitter. You can relieve this fear, by telling the owner that this is typical puppy behavior, and you are a professional. You can handle it. Not only that, you should mention that you do puppy training, and that you can improve this dog's behavior. Sell your puppy training!

When I shake the client's hand, I grab the hand with both hands. This tells the client that they are special, and that I value their business and friendship.

When I haven't seen a client dog in a while, I tell the client that I miss her dog. This is schmoozing. But it's not insincere, because I truly do love these dogs, and it shows in my words and my actions. If it's not sincere it will sound wrong.

Not all clients are equal in importance.

Some clients have given me tens of thousands of dollars in business. So I treat them extra special. I remember their birthday, and I give them special status, and do favors for them, whenever possible, to show them that I appreciate their business.

If I was selling vacuum cleaners, I would not be able to do schmoozing to the level that I'm talking about. You can't fall in love with a vacuum cleaner, or get excited about vacuum cleaning. But you can lose your heart to the soft eyes of a puppy, and you can bond with a dog in an almost magical way. So I am a reflection of these qualities of the dogs, and the owners that love them so much.

For me, dog sitting is an attitude of extreme positivity and friendliness, cooperation and safety, play times and dog walks, puppy training and nap times. It's an excellent job and I wouldn't trade it for anything.

I have the best boss in the world, because I'm self-employed. And I have the best co-workers in the world, because they are all dogs.

ᘖ(˙·౪·˙)υ

Your Attitude as a Dog Professional

The first thing I want to say is, don't lose your cool!

Dogs can be frustrating at times. Dogs are going to test your patience, and if you lose your cool, I promise you will regret it.

The first thing you must realize as a new dog professional, is your neighbors are always watching you. I don't care if you live in a small town or a big city,

your neighbors are watching you. This is 2020, and everyone has a camera.
Everyone is aware of what their neighbors are doing. Don't be stupid. If you
are upset, you need to go sit down and cool off. Do some meditation, deep
breathing, go take a cold shower, do something to lose that irritation and
frustration. Do not bring that stuff to work. And if a dog upsets you, put him
in a time out, and go cool off. Don't come back to that dog until you are
mentally cool and stable.

You must always pick up your dog poop.

There are rare exceptions when you simply cannot pick it up safely.
Examples would be if the dog is pooping in the dark, or poops on snow and
ice, or if he poops in a busy intersection of traffic, or if he poops in autumn
leaves and you simply can't see the poop. But again I want you to remember
that your neighbors are watching you. If you leave poop on the sidewalk or
street, people will see you and notice, and rumors will spread. I always have
more poop bags on my person then I need for the day. It is unacceptable to
be caught without a poop bag.

Some people feel like it's wrong to put a bag of poop in the trash can of one
of your neighbors. I don't feel this way. I will respect my neighbor's
property but if they have their trash can on the curb, and I have a bag of poop
in my hands, it's better to put it in their trash can, then it is to just leave it on
their lawn. I've been doing this for many, many years, and never once has
anyone complained about me putting poop in their can.

Sometimes there is no residential trash cans to use, and I have to use a
business trash can. If the trash can is one of those big green dumpsters that is
usually behind a gate, I will open the gate ,and put the poop in the big trash
can, and close the gate again. I need to be civil and respectful to my
neighbors, because my neighbors are my customers and potential customers.

When you are walking a dog or puppy, and they do something incorrect, like
sniffing the lawn for poo or pee, barking at at passing dog, or trying to walk
behind you so that the leash winds around your feet, I don't think you should
be using rough corrections by jerking on the leash.

I feel like this could hurt the vertebrae in the neck of the dog. I am not a big
fan of leash corrections that call for yanking on the leash. I don't want to

cause neck injuries to a dog, and if you snap a dog's neck even by accident, it will probably ruin your entire dog business. Be smart. If a dog is that crazy and wild and unrestrained on a leash walk, you should be using the prong collar. The prong collar requires no rough corrections. The prong collar is in itself a rough correction but it's done with the dogs energy, and not yours. You are much stronger than a dog. If the dog jumps at the leash, his own body momentum will be the correction on the prong collar.

Normally I don't say many verbal corrections when I'm walking on the leash.

That's because I want the dog to understand that the pattern and routine of leash walking is not something exceptional, but something routine. It doesn't require a command, because it's the normal thing to do.

I will say "No!" If the dog is doing something impeding the walk, like walking behind me, or taking too long to sniff a spot on the grass. If I am making a turn to the left or right, I will let the dog know by saying "Come!"

Occasionally a dog will look at me as if he is unsure what to do next. I will make eye contact with him and say, "Good dog!", and put my hand to his nose, so he can feel my energy is calm and focused. Then we resume the walk.

You should always be friendly on walks. When I see a stranger and his dog, I will usually greet the dog with a smile like this, "Hi Labrador!" Or "Hi Corgi!" This type of greeting will put the owner at ease, and put the dog at ease, because I am a friendly voice and face.

I always carry pepper spray, in my front left pocket, when I walk my dogs.

I've never had to use it, but I started dog sitting in the Detroit and Flint areas. In those cities, there are so many pit bulls, many of them strays, living on the street, super dangerous, and super wild.

I have a responsibility to protect my dogs, and I will used to pepper spray, and my feet, and whatever else it takes, to make sure my dogs are safe.

If you are confronted with a pit bull and he attacks, you want to keep your dog close to you. This way you can protect your dog. You want to start shouting loudly and aggressively, immediately, to draw public attention to the wild dog, and to intimidate the dog, and hopefully get it to change its mind.

You have to be willing to use your feet to defend your dog. Use that pepper spray before the dog gets close enough to bite. I recommend you practice using the pepper spray on a tree trunk, or another target, once a month, to make sure you can hit your target quickly, and to make sure your pepper spray does not get clogged, old, or empty.

When you are walking dogs on the leash, do not cross the street when it's busy.

People are crappy drivers. They may see you, because you are 6ft tall, but if you're walking a dog who is 6 inches off the ground, and the wrong color, they can easily miss your dog and run right over her.

I wait until it's really safe to cross, and then I trot across. Dogs that I walk regularly, have grown familiar with my trotting across the street. They all trot across the street now.

I want them to have a mild fear of the street, because if they ever find themselves unsupervised and on the streets, I want them to stay away from cars and streets.

I always answer my phone calls, when they are from a client that is already saved in my phone as a contact. But in this business, I get a tsunami of robocalls and automated calls, trying to sell me health insurance, warranty plans for my refrigerator, and all sorts of garbage.

I let an unrecognized phone call go to my voicemail, if it's not saved in my contacts.

I have an app on my smartphone it translates my voice calls into a text message, that I receive by email. This allows me to answer the call at my convenience. If I'm walking dogs and a new client calls, I can't handle the distraction of talking to someone on the phone, while walking a dog through a busy city.

It is better to handle the call when I get back home, and I have my clipboard and pen with me, so I can write down the details and notes. So my recommendation is to let calls go to voicemail, if they are from unidentified callers.

The attitude of the dog professional is one of Safety First. Security is tight and I am always thinking about security and safety.

The attitude of a dog pro is one of heavy marketing. But the good news is, you don't have to be a great marketer, because you have a great service. Dogs are universally loved by most people, and definitely loved by all of your clients. Show pictures of dogs in all your marketing, because they are naturally photogenic, super lovable, and you can't find a better mascot for your business than a cute puppy.

You should have a genuine love for dogs to be in this business. The Love Is different from the owner loving her dog. This is a love that requires you to sometimes practice "tough love", which means to make a dog uncomfortable in order to teach the dog of valuable lesson. You will always apply discomfort to a dog with compassion, common sense, and safety.

If you are using discomfort to train a dog, and it is obvious after many attempts that the dog did not learn the lesson, it is unethical for you to continue using painful techniques if it is obvious they're not working.

Don't torture the dog. If you are frustrated, you can seek the advice of another dog trainer online, or download a dog training book. There are tons of YouTube videos on every possible dog problem, and if you message me using the email at the back of this book, you can ask me anything, and I will give you professional advice, free of charge. I just want your business to succeed.

ϛ(￣ ⁔ ￣)ʊ

Training Videos

There are two types of training videos and want to talk about.

The first type is professional level training videos that you might find on YouTube, or maybe you purchased a special training video online. You should be very familiar with all training techniques, even ones you do not currently approve of, or practice. The reason is because you need to sound knowledgeable when discussing training with clients. If they mention a training technique, and you look baffled, they will quickly assume that you don't know what you're talking about.

Sometimes a client will ask me questions about training, but their dog may be too old for me to accept in the puppy training program.

In that event, I might send the client a link to my professional level videos, so they can solve the problem themselves, at home.

For example, if a client calls me and says they have a 2 year old Schnauzer who it's still not housebroken, I would not want that dog in my home because if he hasn't learned housebreaking in two years, it might be impossible to teach him. In this situation I would send the client a link to my Dropbox. The link would connect to my best housebreaking video. That's the best I can do to help that person, really.

The next training videos I want to talk about are the ones I make myself, starring the puppies I am currently training.

I usually make two videos initially, one when I'm walking the dog for the first time, and one when I'm training the dog for basic commands for the very first time. I will post these videos on YouTube and my Facebook page. It is good public relations, and it reminds people that I do puppy training.

Then, when the dog is graduating, I will make two more exit videos, showing the dramatic Improvement in basic commands and leash walking. I will also post these on Facebook and YouTube.

About once a week, I will post a video on YouTube, where I am training the puppy for basic commands. I want the client to be part of the training process, and weekly videos is the minimum.

When you post your own videos on Facebook and YouTube, you should "like" your own videos. I know that sounds cheesy, but if you don't like the videos, you shouldn't expect anyone else to either. When I like a video on Facebook, I use the "heart" emoji like, that represents love, because I truly do love these dogs and I want the whole world to know that.

Let's talk about what you don't want to do in a training video. You never want to correct the dog firmly in a video, as that is suicide for your business. You never want to make a video in a dirty house. Clean your house! You never want to make a video with dogs barking or whining in the background.

If the dog is uninterested in training, or is refusing to participate or listen to your commands, don't post that garbage video. That video is evidence of your poor training, and you never want to post anything like that. I recommend you practice the training for a few days, and then post a better video of the dog performing the commands perfectly.

ʕ•̫͡•ʔ

Pricing Your Services

Perhaps you are wondering how I arrived at the $50,000 a year salary.

If I lived in a big city, I would have my house at full capacity, which would be 10 dogs. I charge $25 a day per dog, so that's $250 a day. It really doesn't matter if the dogs are here for puppy training, or for dog sitting, because the charge is basically the same. Don't tell my puppy training clients that!

If I have 10 dogs that is $250 a day, x 365 days a year, comes to over $91,000. So $50,000 is well within reach. When I have only five dogs in my home, I call that a slow day. I am currently training two puppies at a time, but I recommended you start with just one puppy, until you master the puppy training process. Two puppies can drive you crazy if you're new at this.

I live in a small farm town with less than 10,000 people in it. People here do not vacation as often as people in big cities. In fact, many of my neighbors have never left the town their whole lives.

For that reason, there is less vacation traffic here. If you live in a big city you can easily make more than I do in this small farm town.

I charge $25 a day for overnight dog sitting, or for Doggy Daycare.

People think I should charge less for doggy day care, but the hassle of getting up in the morning to receive the dog, and doing the same in the evening to release the dog, makes it almost the same effort. If I have a client who is struggling financially, I may give them a discount, if they are using my service frequently.

Another income stream that makes me between $1,000 and $2,000 a year is therapy dog training. I charge $250 to train a dog to be a certified therapy dog. I schedule nursing home visits in the afternoon when things are slow, and I take the therapy dog training to the nursing home for an hour. The dog gets petted by nurses and residents, and I take pictures and post them on my Facebook page for therapy dogs. I also share that link on my main dog sitting Facebook page, to remind friends that I train therapy dogs.

So how did I arrive at the $25 a day price? My main competition can be found easily on Rover.com. I simply go on there and I type in my ZIP code, and I see what people are charging near me. Some people charge $30 a day, and other people charge $20 a day. Anyone charging more than $30 is an idiot, and anyone charging under $20 is a safety risk for the dog. If I see trends changing I will boost my price up a bit.

When I raise my prices, I don't like to raise the price of a current client. So what I do is, going forward, with new clients, I introduce the new rate. This policy creates client loyalty, just like rent control in New York City.

It's not as easy to figure out the best price for your puppy training. That's because few people are offering the puppy boot camp.

I feel that $500 to $600 is a good price, for 3 weeks of puppy training, and the Canine Good Citizen Award, and most importantly the housebreaking, which no one else offers.

Right now I am in a price transition with my puppy training. I charge some clients $600 but other clients may get $500. Usually the one to get the lower price are breeders that I work with. I don't want to spook them by telling them I raised my prices.

My Facebook page clearly shows my rates. $25 a day for dog sitting or Doggy Daycare, and $600 for 3 week puppy boot camp. By disclosing my price honestly, people know what to expect from my service. Also, if I want to close a puppy training client on the phone, I may mention that it is normally $600 on my Facebook page but I'm offering them a discount if they commit now. I don't like to use hard sale tactics, because this is not the type of business that justifies it. My feeling is, since no one else is offering housebreaking service, I am the only game in town. That's why people have come from as far as Canada for me to train their puppy, and from other states as well.

When you discuss your price, you state it as if you were stating a simple fact, like what color your hair is.

You don't emphasize or stumble on the price, you just mention it, and then talk about what services you are providing. If it's puppy training, it will sound like this... "I offer a 3-week puppy training boot camp, where the puppy lives with me, so I can give him 24/7 guidance and support. I teach him housebreaking, the most difficult lesson of all, and something 99% of dog trainers won't provide. I will teach the dog the following commands, Sit, Stay, Come, Down, No, Quiet, Go Pee. I will teach the dog to get along well with other friendly dogs, and to walk on the leash correctly. I will help your puppy break bad habits like barking, chewing, digging, jumping up, whining, nipping, mouthing, etc. On graduation, your puppy will receive the Canine Good Citizen Award. I will give you a detailed progress report at graduation, covering every step of the training, so you can continue the puppy's progress when you get home."

When I am selling my dog sitting service, on the phone, the conversation might sound like this... "I have a big fenced yard and a doggie door, so the dogs can come in and out anytime they like. This is a home atmosphere, but not a kennel. I don't crate dogs unless I am puppy training or unless they need it for their own safety. I have plenty of dog beds, and the dogs are allowed to sleep on the couch as well. All dogs in my home get free daily walks, and I will send you pictures and videos of your dog so you know she is safe and happy.

ʖ(¯· ﻌ ¯·)ʋ

Yard Signs for Special Clients

An excellent way to get new business is using yard signs. Here's how you want to do it.

It doesn't help you to put a yard sign in your own yard. All your neighbors already know you are a dog sitter, and a puppy trainer, so this sign does not help you.

What you want to do is develop special relationships with clients, who have a high regard for you and your business. I have a few really good friends who love dogs so much, and we bond because of our mutual love for dogs. These friends are like super good fans of my business, so I feel totally comfortable asking them to put a $20 yard sign in their front yard.

Now all of their neighbors are going to see my yard sign, advertising dog sitting and puppy training, showing my phone number, and a picture of a very cute puppy. No more information is necessary. I recommend you get a double sided sign for better visibility.

Double sided yard signs in full color, and totally customizable text and images, are available for under $20 at Vistaprint.

The cool thing about the yard sign is you can make it look very humble. The sign should look like it's just a small business, or even a side hustle. People don't want to come to a Walmart-size business for something so personal as dog sitting. They love the personal connection.

Make your sign friendly and super simple. I strongly recommend the sign say, "Dog Sitting__ Puppy Training__ and your phone number." Add a picture of the cutest puppy you can find online, and your sign is ready to go.

The reason you should use an online photo, rather than your own, is because you want the highest quality picture for a sign. The lighting, and picture quality might not be super if you are using your smartphone.

Sometimes a client will tell you how much they are grateful for your service. When they start singing praises, that's the perfect time to ask them if you can put a yard sign in their front yard. This makes it so easy to do highly effective marketing in new areas.

If your client lives very far away, like more than 50 miles away, don't advertise a yard sign for dog sitting. That's too far. But you can still advertise for puppy training.

In some elite communities, city zoning may not allow residential yard signs.

If that's the case, no big deal, just pick up your sign, and save it in your basement, for the next time a client is singing your praises. You will thank the client for her kind words, and ask her if you can put a yard sign in her front lawn.

The yard sign is one of the most effective marketing strategies you will ever use.

ϟ(¯ ᴗ ¯)ʋ

Saving Dog Clients In My Phone

When a potential dog client calls me, I don't really have any need to ask them for their last name. I will ask them for their first name, and the name of the dog.

Then I will save them in my phone, as a contact, after I hang up from the conversation. Let's say Sarah calls me, and she has a two-year-old Schnauzer named Lola. I will save her in my phone as "Sarah dog Lola". This way, when she calls me in a month or two, I can answer by saying, "Hi Sarah! How is Lola doing?"

If a caller is asking me for information only, and we are not ready to exchange names and personal information, I save them in my phone as "dog caller". This way, when they call later, I know they are not a telemarketer or robocall. I know that they are at least mildly interested in doing dog business with me.

There is a spot on your contact information of your smartphone, where you can put the person's address. I usually use this area to note any important information about the dog. If the dog is aggressive, or sick, or needs medication, or if I gave the client a special price, I will make those notes in the address section of the contact.

The truth is, I don't care about a person's last name. My business is a cash-based business, so I don't have a need for someone's last name. I also don't share my last name with many people, because it's not necessary for them to know that.

I am known as Alex the Dog Sitter, or Alex the Puppy Trainer. My last name does not help anyone make a decision to do business with me. But my profession as a dog sitter does help people decide to do business with me, so I am constantly referring to myself as Alex the Puppy Trainer or Alex the Dog Sitter.

By the way, notice I say Dog Sitter, and not Pet Sitter. I am not a pet sitter lol, I don't watch cats or birds, I think it would be very unfair to put a cat in a house with a bunch of dogs! You are a dog sitter, and if you say you are a pet sitter, someone is going to ask you to watch their horse, or their goat, or maybe their snake!

If I save a dog in my phone, and the owner gets a second dog that I am working with, I will put the new dog name first in order. This way, when I'm looking on my phone to send a picture to the owner, I will see the new dog's name and not the old dog's name. Remember, dogs don't live very long, so you will sometimes have to delete a dog's name who has passed away, and replace it with the new dog. Very sad.

Your smartphone is your main tool in your dog business. I do not advise you to get an iPhone but if you already have an iPhone you will just have to make do with it. The Android is more flexible and has broader applications in my opinion. Don't skimp on memory or speed or Wi-Fi. You are running a business on your phone, so make sure your phone is strong enough to handle the load.

ʕ(ˉ ᴥ ˉ)ᴅ

Therapy Dogs

I make it least $1,000 a year off therapy dogs. I have my own Facebook page specifically for therapy dog training.

I charge $250 to train a person's dog to be a certified therapy dog. That means I do approximately 4 dogs a year as therapy dogs. I charge $25 a visit to a nursing home near me. I take the dogs there for a half hour to an hour. They are greeted and petted by the nursing staff and the residents, they wear their little red vest with the *therapy dog* words printed on the side, and it's a really happy and fun activity for them, and for me.

I do not certify through the AKC for the therapy dog title. The reason why is because the AKC has a lot of difficult requirements for the therapy dog title. For example, they want 50 facility visits to a nursing home or similar place. If I had to charge one client 50 visits, that would be $1,250 and none of my clients could afford that.

So what I do, is I explain that my certification is just through my dog business. I make up for it by giving them a beautiful rosewood plaque that I order from the local trophy shop. When the therapy dog graduates from my training program, I get their picture taken and placed on the rosewood plaque, with their name and *Certified Therapy Dog* title. The plaque looks beautiful and the owners love it. It is much more impressive than a piece of paper from AKC.

When I'm considering a dog for therapy dog training, I am very careful.

I want a dog who is friendly, likes to be petted, obedient, and definitely housebroken. If the dog is all these things, he is a good candidate for therapy dog training.

Most candidates for therapy dog training are what I called 99 percenters. They are great dogs, but they are not perfect for therapy dogs. For example, let's say a Great Dane wants to be a therapy dog, but he moves in such a way that he could knock over at elderly person in a nursing home and break a hip. I would think very hard about rejecting that dog for therapy dog training because of the risk involved.

Dogs who are not perfectly housebroken, or aggressive in any way, even barking, are not a good fit for this. A dog that you don't trust to be off leash, might be a concern as a therapy dog.

On a therapy dog visit, I will take the dog in my car to the nursing home, check in at the front gate, and walk around, introducing the dog to the nursing staff who always are so friendly and lovable to the dogs. If the nurses are dog owners, I am always quick to give them my business card for dog sitting or puppy training.

The nurses are so helpful and friendly in the nursing home. The residents are also friendly, but some suffer from dementia, and others are just trapped in mild depression, etc. Be careful and make sure your dog is safe and that you are safe. I usually ask a senior, "Do you like dogs?" If they say "No" I wish them a nice day and move away.

When I am in the nursing home, I am not allowed to take pictures of the face of any residents. So I make sure I only take pictures of the dogs, and not a headshot of the residents.

When I get home after the therapy dog visits, I will post the pictures on my Facebook page for therapy dogs, and I will share the link to my main dog sitting site. This way I am reminding my dog sitting clients that I also train therapy dogs.

My dogs Katie and Clover are both therapy dogs. When I introduce them to people, they notice the good behavior, and I mentioned that they are therapy dogs. This has led to a number of new business opportunities.

The nurses at the nursing home, are some of my best clients. They all seem to be dog lovers and dog owners, and it is really good public relations for me to be seen in there, bringing therapy dogs on a regular basis.

There is something magical about seeing a senior smile as he pets your therapy dog, and remembers the dogs he used to own and love in his life.

৬(˘ ૦ ˘)ʋ

Thank You for Buying My Book!